What Are You Thinking?

The Stuff of Wisdom in a Postmodern World

John R. Ingram

Psalm 37:23, 24

by

John R. Ingram

Bloomington, IN   authorHOUSE®   Milton Keynes, UK

AuthorHouse™
1663 Liberty Drive, Suite 200
Bloomington, IN 47403
www.authorhouse.com
Phone: 1-800-839-8640

AuthorHouse™ UK Ltd.
500 Avebury Boulevard
Central Milton Keynes, MK9 2BE
www.authorhouse.co.uk
Phone: 08001974150

First published by AuthorHouse 2/19/2007

ISBN: 1-4259-4815-4 (sc)

Library of Congress Control Number: 2006907218

Printed in the United States of America
Bloomington, Indiana

This book is printed on acid-free paper.

Jesus Said, You will know the truth and the truth will set you free
How Do We Know the Truth?
What is Truth?

"You are a king, then!" said Pilate. Jesus answered, "You are right in saying I am a king. In fact, for this reason I was born, and for this I came into the world, to testify to the truth. Everyone on the side of truth listens to me." "What is truth?" Pilate asked. With this he went out again to the Jews and said, "I find no basis for a charge against him" John 18:37,38).

Dedication

To

My bride, my friend, my love, my helpmate,

Sharon,

My wife of 42 years

Whose unwavering commitment to Christ

Has challenged me in my thinking

Foreword

James Thurber, in his volume of satire, *Let Your Mind Alone*, recalls that during 1929 when the Great Depression began, Walter B. Pitkin announced, "for the first time in the career of mankind happiness is coming within the reach of millions of people."[1] Pitkin's view was that six or seven persons out of every ten could attain happy living, but that only one person in a thousand was actually reaching that goal. According to Pitkin, the obstacles standing in the way of the remaining nine hundred and ninety-nine unhappy ones was they did not know themselves, did not understand the "science of happiness" and had no "Technique of Thinking." It is apparent from the title of Thurber's book he did not agree with Pitkin's evaluation of the times. Thurber's assessment after referring to many "success experts" of the day was "man will be better off if he quits monkeying with his mind and just lets it alone."[2]

Thurber may have found greater homogeneity in today's world. Our postmodern world has a similar direction; instead of attempting to make sense out of philosophy, art and literature let's just celebrate 'nonsense.' The current postmodern belief is that a correct description of Reality is impossible. Truth is limited, constantly evolving and no theory can ever be proven true or explain all things. Therefore celebrate the 'freedom' from trying to make sense of anything. It goes without saying that underlying contemporary thought is a broad band of skepticism.

Often the philosophy of both the Christian and the non-Christian is akin to Thurber's conclusion. It is often expressed in such terms as, "Religion is a personal matter" or "I never discuss religion or politics." Although we may claim to 'know' our own minds, the mind is still very mysterious. "How do we know?" "What is the process of knowing?" What is it in my Psyche that guides decision-making? In an age of incredible advancement in technology, especially in the area of communication, with global information at our fingertips -as close as the web browser on our computer- it seems that we have not made any great strides in understanding how to think. In the area of understanding faith, unfortunately for many it has become something relegated to the area of experience and emotion, subjective and totally divorced from reason.

In this work I want to acknowledge Dr. J. Barton Payne, a scholar, a gentleman, a gracious Christian, A humble professor, a mentor, one I considered my friend, who taught me how to think. His untimely death in the seventies took him to be with the Lord he worshipped and adored. His passing left a great void.

It is the earnest desire of this author that the journey taken in these pages will lead to an understanding of the revelation of God's truth, which can give clarity to the mind and escort the seeker to a coherent world and life view. Thinking patterns of the world continue to be hazy and ambiguous. God has provided a path to find His truth and to have guided and focused thinking in all of life's decisions.

John Ingram

Endnotes

[1] James Thurber, "Let Your Mind Alone. Harper & Brothers Publishers, New York:1937, p. 3.

[2] Ibid.

Contents

1
The Stuff Of Wisdom

Measuring Life

Value is often measured in terms of dollars and cents, forgetting that what matters most in life is not found in the market place. For many, hard work and toil is the totality of life. The potential end product of earthly labor is a few material gains. Material focus is compounded with the pressure of performance. Charles Reich, in 1987, identified three levels of consciousness existing in our society, one being the "loss of self" or the sacrifice of individuality to the corporate "good." Success and love is measured by how well you perform. The play, "Portnoy's Complaint" graphically portrays the struggle against the performance-oriented world. Love is received only for accomplishments according to society's terms. The ever-present danger for the performer is taking one wrong step and slipping beneath the thin veneer of success into "an abyss...where one becomes a non-person."[3] The recent "Survivor" series on television seems to support this emphasis and bombards us with the philosophy that it really is winning that counts, not how you run the race.

Sadly, within the realm of professing Christian ministries many are also subject to the performance-value system, fearful of not measuring up to self-imposed or church-imposed standards of "excellence." Many churches have made meticulous methods, not ministry the holy grail of faith. True biblical faith challenges us to step off the performance treadmill and take stock of our relationship with God and with people. The bible is not a guide to excellence in spiritual performance.

In the midst of our daily efforts, sometimes little thought is given to moving beyond the monotony of the moment. The song by the group, Alabama, gets right to the heart of what many are feeling:

I'm in a hurry to get things done oh I,
rush and rush until life's no fun.
All I really gotta' do is live and die
But I'm in a hurry and don't know why.[4]

Performance orientation leads ultimately to burnout. There is a better way of thinking that leads to restive and exhilarating contentment in the midst of life's storm. There is reality beyond our physical routine that is not a realm of fantasy. Can this reality be reached by human effort and determination alone? Can the wholeness of life be reached apart from power and insight beyond ourselves? A modern philosopher asks this question: "Can we understand the whole of things?" He directs the reader to the viewpoint some hold that we may have a theory of *anything*, but not a theory of *everything*. He observes that such a theory would have to be too general and must come from a standpoint outside the world.[5]

When we delve into these questions of life, we are indulging in philosophy. What is philosophy? Philosophers have struggled with this question throughout the ages. The author of *Modern Philosophy* (1995) makes the astute observation that the history of philosophy has been one long search for its own definition.[6] Perhaps a better way to answer the question, or arrive at a definition, is to ask, "What is the subject matter of philosophy?" The following answer may prick a few ears of the scientific world: "Philosophy studies everything. It tries to define a theory of the *whole* of things. In contrast, to the 'bittiness' of science, philosophy attempts an integrated account of the world, in which all truth will be harmonized."[7] Many so-called philosophers disagree; they want to make science the God of all life, moving it beyond the realm of analytical investigation to become the harmonizer and dictator of all truth.

Although an excellent synopsis of philosophy, the same author abrogates religion to the realm of myth and storytelling, believing the primary goal of religion and moral interpretation is not truth, but consolation.[8] The one discipline that has hope of bringing a prospective to philosophy from beyond the realm of human experience becomes a scrap on the philosopher's cutting floor. A. J. Ayer, in his book, *Philosophy in the Twentieth Century,* expresses this divorce of religion and philosophy:

> ...the common belief that 'it is the business of the philosopher to tell men how they ought to live, although it has the authority of Plato, is based upon a fallacy. The mistake is that of supposing that morality is a subject like geology, or art-history, in which there are degrees of expertise, so that just as one can look to an art-historian, in virtue of his training, to determine whether some picture is a forgery, one can look to a philosopher to determine whether some action is wrong. The philosopher has no such training, not because of any defect in his education but because there is no such thing as an authoritative guide to moral judgment, of which he could have obtained the mastery.[9]

Understanding of life *is* the work of philosophy. We cannot put together all the pieces of life merely by our human experience. If in fact there is no such thing as an "authoritative guide to moral judgment," then any discussion of philosophy is futile. True wisdom must come from someone who transcends our mortal existence. Philosophy derives from two Greek words, that may be interpreted, "love of wisdom." God want us to know His wisdom. Solomon, credited with being a man of great perception, wrote, "For the Lord gives wisdom, and from his mouth come knowledge and understanding."[10] Thinkers throughout history have searched for the "stuff of wisdom." Unfortunately, many have not been willing to seek the One who has a viewpoint from beyond our world and can see the whole.

It is difficult to see life beyond our environment and day-by-day existence without understanding the process of thinking. Thinking involves more that daydreaming. Man was created to know God, and have a true understanding of life. God wants to lead us to that insight. The path will lead to a spiritual connection of faith and reason. Although mankind now struggles with the blindness of a sinful nature, God has provided a way back to His wisdom. The apostle Paul wrote, "Do not conform any longer to the pattern of this world, but be transformed by the renewing of your mind. Then you will be able to test and approve what God's will is—his good, pleasing and perfect will."[11]   Paul speaks of renewing the *rational* mind. God wants to redeem us from confusion, bring clarity to thinking, and restore our rational minds with solid faith. God offers the opportunity of studying His divine truth so we can make sense of life, and not be tossed to and fro upon the stormy sea of experience.

"How do we know truth?" Mankind was originally deceived into thinking that it was possible to have the true wisdom of God by disobedience; that God was withholding his wisdom from the very ones created in His likeness. This was the beginning of Gnostic belief; believing there is somehow hidden special knowledge that will connect us with wisdom and make us gods. This was the beginning of confusion not wisdom. That confusion still reigns today in this very complex postmodern world and confounds both skeptical scholars as well as spiritual seekers. The prating political Pilate who turned Jesus over to be crucified struggled with this perplexity. He confronted the one who is the origin of all wisdom: "You are a king, then!" said Pilate. Jesus answered, "You are right in saying I am a king. In fact, for this reason I was born, and for this I came into the world, to testify to the truth. Everyone on the side of truth listens to me." "What is truth?" Pilate asked. With this he went out again to the Jews and said, "I find no basis for a charge against him" (John 18:37,38). Though dubious of finding truth, Pilate could not find anything false in the one who stood before him. Pilate could only acknowledge the complete absence of deception in Jesus Christ.

Thinking Questions

1. How would you measure the value of life?

2. Do you believe it is possible to understand all of reality?

3. Do we know what is reality?

4. What value does science bring to understanding the value of life?

5. Do you believe it is possible to have an authoritative moral guide to all moral issues?

6. Do you understand your own thinking process? How you make decisions?

7. Have you ever asked the question, "What is truth?"

8. Read John chapter 18 and discuss Pilate's view of truth? What world pressures do you believe influenced his thinking?

Endnotes

3   Charles Reich, "The Greening of America, p. 68.

4   Alabama, Copyright © 1998 - 2006 Lerenti.com . All Rights Reserved.

5   Roger Scruton. Modern Philosophy: An introduction and Survey. Allen Lane The Penguin Press, New York, NY, 1995, p. 7

6   Ibid, p. 3.

7   Ibid, p.7

8   Ibid., p.65

9   A.J.Ayer, "Philosophy in the Twentieth Century. Random House, New York: 1982, p. 15

10   Proverbs 2:6

11   Romans 12:2

2
What Were You Thinking?

When my wife and I lived in Canada in 1978, we attended a seminar led by Bruce Scott, called the "Spilling Over"[12] seminar. He identified three levels of communication, which are verbal responses in our thinking process. The first level, "mouth to mouth" is very superficial communication. This is the casual greeting, such as "Hello, how are you?" "Fine!" The second is "head to head" communication; the intellectual exchange that takes place when we may be discussing politics or religious subjects. It involves the mind, but there is not a strong personal connection with the recipient. The third level is "heart to heart" communication. This level not only involves the intellect, but the emotional, feeling level of our being.

Scott's instruction focused on "heart to heart." He emphasized that if we are to reach another person it must be when they have opened up to the "heart to heart" level of communication. At the "mouth to mouth" or "head to head" level we are not really connecting. This may also be applied to our subject of "thinking." The level at which we open the lines of communication to others is a choice. We decide just how vulnerable we will be by the level of communication we permit. In the same fashion, we decide on the thought process by which we view life. It may be very superficial, like "mouth to mouth," it may be an intellectual process like "head to head" without strong personal commitment, or it may involve our very being, like "heart to heart."

The makeup of our heart and mind, created by God, corresponds to faith plus reason. Some want to place faith in the basket of feeling. It involves feeling, but it is not the source. True faith is founded in the will. Reason comes from the mind created in the image of God. Only the creator can properly link faith and reason so we may understand the wholeness of life.

Coming to the place of "heart to heart" in thinking and communication is very difficult. It makes you feel defenseless and vulnerable. It is fear of the helplessness of vulnerability that closes our minds to the struggle to find truth. It is also a fear of rejection. So before delving into more technical aspects of thinking, this author is going to take the first plunge into the heart level. I will dare to share some personal life experiences that God used in my thinking process. After reading some of them, you may want to ask, "John, What *were* you thinking?

It should be obvious that I am not promoting myself as one who has always set definitive goals in my life because of clear thinking. I have had many struggles and sundry experiences, recognize I have made many mistakes, and have not always taken the right fork in the road. Some of those forks have been as a teacher, pastor, truck driver, naval air controlman, draftsman, electrical and instrumentation engineer, automobile service manager, and yes, even a salesman. I would not want anyone to struggle through the same diversities. It is hoped that by sharing these events it will help you to honestly evaluate your thinking and begin considering the wisdom of God in the daily choices of life. This journey into the realm of reflection and thinking will hopefully lead you to understand that the wisdom of faith is both a head and a heart decision.

Tripping along the Path of Life

My senior year in high school in the late spring of 1957 was a pivotal time in my life. I spent a great deal of time with a buddy, named Jim. My friend had a 1951 metallic dark green Oldsmobile, two-door hardtop, beautifully customized with a "rocket V-8" engine; a teenage boys' dream! The day before we graduated from West High School, in Columbus, Ohio, we spent the morning and early afternoon replacing a motor mount. When the repair was finished, we were feeling really pumped and ready to go 'cruising.' We went to a gas station a short distance from my home and put two dollars of gas in the car –which in that era purchased around 16 gallons! We were riding high, ready to rock! We drove back towards my home. I was riding shotgun with my hand out the window, gripping the top of the car. We started to pass a street, when suddenly, from the corner of my eye, I saw that a 1947 Buick was entering the same intersection from our right, and about to crash into my door. Jim saw it also, and in an attempt to avoid the collision, stomped on the accelerator to get past the intersection and avoid the crash. He almost made it; the Buick crashed into our right rear fender. The force of the impact in combination with acceleration caused the car to erratically swerve to the right, hitting the opposite curb. This caused the car to begin to roll, not sideways, but end-to-end, in what seemed to its two-stunned passengers, slow motion, until finally landing upside-down on a front lawn. In the process, the car rolled on my extended hand and ground my face into the dirt.

When the car finally came to rest, I miraculously found myself outside sitting on the ground leaning against the inverted car. I shook myself, called out for Jim and received no answer. I stood up, walked around the car, and there on the opposite side, was Jim, sitting leaning against his door! He spoke to me, and I remember saying, "I think we're in shock." "We better lay down."

Whereas the time for the car to roll over and over seemed like an eternity, it took only seconds until a crowd gathered around the car and two stunned boys. One 'brilliant' young man standing there and seeing some blood on Jim's shirt began yelling, "He's hurt!" "Tear his shirt!" Jim and I had just purchased these very nice Ivy League shirts, which we wore roller-skating. Instead of unbuttoning it, someone reached down and ripped off his sleeve, hurting Jim in the process.

My father heard the crash two blocks away at our home. He hurried down the street to the now growing circle of spectators and stood on the outside perimeter. Suddenly, he spotted our shirts and pushed through the crowd to where we were lying on the ground. I sat up and said, "Dad, we're okay." "Don't worry." Two ambulances came soon, and whisked us away, leaving Jim's shoes behind. If we were not injured in the crash, I believe we could have been in the ride to the hospital. The driver, not slowing down on very high railroad tracks bounced me at least a foot above my gurney.

Less than an hour later, we were both walking away from the hospital. Jim was in stocking feet with a very slight bruise on his arm, and I had a bruised hand and knuckles. As rumors have it, however, that was not the story circulated. Jim's car -what was left of it- was towed to a service station not far from our high school. Many class-members saw the remains. Before we arrived at school the next day, to participate in our graduation, we were both being reported as dead. It caused quite a stir on the front steps of West High School when the "two dead boys" walked up and greeted their classmates!

There is nothing like a near death experience to initiate the thinking process. Up to that time, I had no idea or thought of what to do with my life. There was a promised job working for an architectural firm as a draftsman. Beyond that, I did not have a clue. The accident led to thoughts about the brevity and uncertainty of our existence. Perhaps this was the first experience of seriously thinking about the meaning of life. The accident brought about a sudden revelation of my life's lack of focus, which turned my thoughts towards attending a Christian College. Enrollment in the fall led to a course of study in bible and music. Although not knowing the reason, I believed my life had been miraculously spared. A spark of faith was growing; faith that God actually had a plan for me.

College did not immediately give me clarity in God's will. Acting on a whim the summer after my freshman year, Jim and I went to the Columbus naval air reserve station and joined the Navy without any consultation with God or parents. This spur of the moment decision caused me to give up college seven months later and take a two year world cruise, compliments of the US Navy. In spite of my lack of direction and snap decision, those two years allowed God to do a number on me and open my mind to a thought process regarding His will for my life.

Before that process could begin, one more event clouded my thinking. The following semester, during my sophomore year, I met a girl, and I fell in love. In addition to my love life, I was carrying fifteen hours of classes and working 40 hours at night in a local factory. I began to miss monthly reserve meetings. December, 1958, I went to my girlfriend's home for Christmas and began discussing marriage. I became totally focused on my relationship with her, not considering God's direction. It was that holiday time when an official letter arrived from the Columbus Naval Air Station. March of the following year, I would begin active duty because of the missed meetings. The direction in my life seemed totally at sea (pardon the pun).

I felt the tension with the girl I wanted to marry; leaving her behind for two years and not knowing whether it was right to expect a commitment from her while I was gone. We agreed to wait for each other, and the agony of separation began. That first year, I received letters written daily, as our ship traveled the Atlantic and throughout the Mediterranean Sea. I counted the days until returning on leave, to become officially engaged and perhaps marry.

Shortly before Christmas time, 1959, about nine months into our cruise, our ship entered the Suez Canal from the Mediterranean and was at anchor in the Bitter Lakes region, halfway through the canal. I was standing watch at midnight with the Officer of the Deck. It was 105 degrees, and over the ship's intercom we heard, "Mail Call." I asked permission from the "OD" to go retrieve my mail. Permission being granted, I went to my bunk and picked up the usual letter. Upon tearing it open and starting to read I found a veiled 'Dear John.' She was asking me if it was okay for her to date. She wrote that while I was having such a "good time" seeing all the countries of the world she was very lonely. That 'good time' included seeing eight shipmates die in less than 9 months. Earlier that week on duty in the tower, I saw a sailor walk through a spinning airplane propeller and could not warn him in time. I was involved in the emergency response and cleanup efforts. Perhaps if I had received her letter while in the comparatively free and secure environment of America, I would have ended the relationship. However, I do not believe there can be any situation where you feel more alone, insecure and vulnerable than being a sailor or service person halfway around the world, sometimes in harms way, in a strange country, controlled by the movement of your ship or military unit. It is not a place for depressing news. I am sure there have been countless similar discouragements among our dedicated troops in the Gulf War and those now serving faithfully in the depressing perils of Iraq. Under the circumstances, the letter was overwhelming. I returned to my watch for three more hours in the heat and feigned politeness to the "OD", continuing to maintain my military stance while my insides were in turmoil. The continual chiding and bantering humor of shipmates that one day I would receive a "Dear John" had come true.

When returning home on leave in March of the following year, the initial reunion was re-assuring. However, the offered engagement ring was later turned down, and our relationship did not improve in spite of frantic 1800-mile weekend road trips from Rhode Island to Ohio throughout the summer. It painfully disintegrated. God was beginning to break through to my heartsick being and speak to me about what should be the center of my life. He would eventually bring someone into my life to change my thinking and my focus.

I returned to college in February of 1961, lonely and suffering from sub-culture shock as I re-entered civilian life. By this time, my ex-girlfriend had a steady relationship with a fellow on campus. I soon returned to my 15 hours of classes each day, and 40 hours of employment. During the nights when I was not working, I walked for hours after dark, crying, praying, and asking God to restore the former relationship. The young man who was partially decapitated on our ship by the blades of a propeller walked into the spinning knives while reading a letter from the girl he loved back home. Being the melancholy personality that I am, sometimes I asked God why that could not have been me.

In those days, the college professors and instructors received very little pay. Some of them also took night jobs to make ends meet. A college coach worked at the factory with me. One evening, when we were taking our supper break, sitting outside in the grass, he suddenly spoke. Coach said that he understood my ex-girl friend was dating a fellow on campus during the week, and I was traveling home with her on weekends and dating her. This was apparently a joke going around the locker room among the jocks. In my emotional state it was devastating; I jumped up, and screamed at him, "She would never do that!" "She is not that kind of girl!" He later came and apologized, but no one ever came alongside of me to help with my inward struggles. I punched my time card and left early that night, returning to campus to resume my façade of everything being okay. I continued trying to 'make sense' of the hurtful events in my life.

As the saying goes, insult was added to injury. The president of our college was also the father of my ex-girl's new steady. A short time after the factory incident, I received a call in the afternoon at my dorm. The president was on the line demanding I come to his office immediately. I arrived there a short time later and walked in greeted by the president and the dean of students. The president began accusing me of speaking out against the school and his policies, an apparent rumor picked up from someone at the library where I helped out on staff. Anyone close to me knew my love and support for the school. Although probably not the motivation, I felt that he was trying to get me off campus because of his son's relationship with my ex. I told him I believed I knew the source of the rumor and must have been correct, because it ended the confrontation. I left the office that day and quickly lost my lunch.

To most on campus, "Johnny" was a happy-go-lucky extrovert, kind of crazy guy, college choir president, and class vice-president, seemingly without problems. During this period, I dated a number of girls, and in most cases ended up hurting them as I fled from any deep relationship. I found a note penned by one of these girls in a returned book years later. It read, "The saddest words of tongue or pen are "It might have been."

Inside I was crying and going through the shock of re-entry into civilian life.

There were no counselors in those days to discuss what I was experiencing. I came from two years in the environment of the military, living aboard ship with 3000 men, great freedom in every port of call, experienced the death of fellow crewmen, saw poverty, degradation, disease, and every sin imaginable in thirteen countries of the world. I had returned to a strict conservative college life, where seemingly the most serious concerns were lights out at 11:00, girls skirts two inches below the knees, and "campusing" for the silliest infractions. There were few teachers in those days that could have, or would have willingly discussed my inward struggles.

Fortunately, and miraculously, somehow in God's sovereign grace and unfathomable wisdom, *disappointment* can become His *appointment*. Somehow He takes our mistakes and misdirection and turns it into new purpose when we let Him take control. As the apostle Paul wrote to the Roman church, "we know that in all things God works for the good of those who love him, who have been called according to his purpose."[13] God, knowing my purpose in life far better than I, brought me together with the girl who was to become my beloved wife. One day, when entering the local church, I heard singing; it was the loveliest soprano voice I had ever heard. I could not wait to see the person attached to that sound. I was not disappointed when I met Sharon.

Our early relationship was stormy, on again, off again, partly because I was afraid of a commitment and afraid of being hurt again. She was a woman who knew her heart and mind, but had her own inward struggles. In spite of those difficulties, she first and foremost wanted to put God first in every relationship. A previous relationship was ended with someone she deeply cared for because she wanted God's will. God knew I needed to be confronted. She challenged me to consider what God's plans were for the future. Once I found a little box, with a tiny note from her. It contained words from Proverbs 22:29, saying that a person diligent (focused) in business will stand before persons of stature. I pulled some silly stunts that would have sent most girls running. She stuck with me even when I spun my car tires in front of the college library throwing mud all over her clothes.

God knew I needed to lighten up and have a little humor in my life. Sharon took advantage of one of my silly 'campusing' episodes; I was grounded in my dorm (lovingly called "Cedar Shack") for a couple of weeks because of a harmless prank. During my "incarceration" she anonymously sent me several humorous cards including a 'coming out' card, with her version of the ballad, "Big Bad John." She wrote,

> The date will be April 4th, 1962, the time is eight hours and counting. From out of that old beat-up building with broken windows and funny things hanging on walls will emerge the figure of that notorious BIG BAD JOHN! To once again take up the natural, free, spacious, out-door life (?) of a run-of-the-mill college student. You will see him staggering out with half-closed eyes, climbing with difficulty into a big Buick, speeding off late to open the library [my work assignment] and stumbling late and out of breath into Greek class. So

once again will begin the old normal life of the one and only- BIG BAD JOHN! The verse was preceded by the words, "Purrr-ty please?" "May I come out now?" And followed after in large letters, "PLEASE DO!"

The following winter, I remember a cold, crisp, snowy night in our small college town. We were walking the streets –everything glistening and sparkling like diamonds- going door-to-door caroling during the Christmas season. Sharon walking by my side slipped her hand into my hand and into my coat pocket to get warm. Somehow at that moment I knew God was filling my heart with a new love. On January 13th, a cold, clear Sunday night, after a mischievous walk from church back to her campus home, I asked her to marry me, and she said yes. She is now my faithful wife and friend of 42 years, through thick and very thin, in spite of 21 moves in our lives, throughout five states and Canada. She never questioned God's call in spite of our trials and difficult hardships along the path of life, continuing to be a devoted mother and faithful spouse.

Finding Focus

How were these two relationships different? Had I truly loved the first girl I planned to marry? Yes. I also truly love Sharon and I am committed to her. The difference was in thinking. Through the first relationship I was trying to find complete fulfillment in another person. That is impossible. Is it possible for two people to find fulfillment in each other? Definitely. But first, there must be a right relationship with the one who created us. He is the only one who can fill the God-shaped vacuum within us. God can enable us to be whole, complete persons apart from any other person, except Him. Only God can bring clarity to our thinking. When that focus is right, it enhances all our other relationships.

For two summers during my college years I drove a large International R-190 truck. This employment filled the summer after my senior year while Sharon traveled with the college trio representing the school. The large 12-ton truck (for me about two steps up to the running board) had no power steering, a two-speed axle, 10 gears, and no synchronization in the transmission. In simple terms, it meant I had to "double clutch" each time I shifted gears. I hauled cylinders of gas (some in excess of 280 pounds) and fifty-pound blocks of dry ice. The work was very heavy, especially for my 5 feet 4 inch frame. Some of the cylinders were taller than me! I replaced a summer driver who was six feet six inches tall. He quit because he could not handle the cylinders. The first two weeks, I also threatened to quit every hour. Then, in an unexpected way, I broke through to winning.

The cylinders did not get any lighter, and I had not yet fully learned the secrets of handling them. The turning point came shortly after sunrise, while at the Central Ohio Breeders Association delivering fifty-pound dry ice blocks and nitrogen cylinders. I was sitting in my truck cab, shaken, after nearly knocking a supporting post out of the building when backing the truck to the loading dock. Looking through the windshield and out across the countryside I was suddenly gripped by the beauty of the country landscape. The rising sun was painting streaks of gold across the sky; the ripening fields were glistening with morning dew, reflecting the morning light. The realization dawned on me that I was free to bask in all the beauty of God's creation while carrying out my toilsome duties and driving from town to town.

Something happened in my spirit. Suddenly the cylinders and dry ice were no longer as heavy; the ten-speed truck with no 'synchros' in the gearbox began to shift without grinding; the job turned from labored to lighthearted. The realization broke through that labor alone should not be my focus. I began to ponder the hills and countryside, the smells of summer, and the beauty of God's creation. As the enlightened view of my immediate circumstances dawned I became emotionally and physically able to handle my labors. Have you every wrapped your arms across your own body in a sense of wanting to feel secure in a frightful or alarming situation? At that moment, in the rather dingy interior of my truck I felt like God wrapped His arms around me and gave me a hug.

A short time after this experience, a letter came from Sharon with these verses from Corinthians: "Therefore, if anyone is in Christ, he is a new creation; the old has gone, the new has come! All this is from God, who reconciled us to himself through Christ and gave us the ministry of reconciliation: that God was reconciling the world to himself in Christ, not counting men's sins against them. And he has committed to us the message of reconciliation."[14] God was gently opening the channels into my mind and heart through the one He chose to be my life partner.

I did not recognize that my world and life view was affected. Nor at the time did I equate this with a shift in my philosophy of life. God was able to break into my routine and let me know there was something far greater than just daily existence. In a world filled with nonsense He can make sense of our existence. Solomon wrote in the book of proverbs, "Wisdom calls aloud in the street, she raises her voice in the public squares; at the head of the noisy streets she cries out, in the gateways of the city she makes her speech."[15] Where is wisdom? How do we find it? Why is it difficult to hear her voice? James the brother of the Lord wrote, "If any of you lacks wisdom, he should ask God, who gives generously to all without finding fault, and it will be given to him."[16]

Is it that simple? If so, then why don't more people find it? Why did a young man struggle for so long to find it? The answer may be as simple as these words of James: "You do not have, because you do not ask God. When you ask, you do not receive because you ask with wrong motives, that you may spend what you get on your pleasures" (James 4:2b, 3). Jesus instructed us how to find it: "So I say to you: Ask and it will be given to you; seek and you will find; knock and the door will be opened to you. For everyone who asks receives; he who seeks finds; and to him who knocks, the door will be opened (Matthew 7:7,8).

If God gets frustrated, he must have had a major aggravation with me; I have always wanted to hit the ground running, but unfortunately, I often just hit the ground. God often had to wake me up with the proverbial two-by-four so I would begin thinking clearly and stop taking giant steps of expediency.

Whatever Works

Often our thinking is based primarily on expediency. A common ability in this modern world appears to be adeptness at self-interest. Many years ago, I met the ultimate expedient person while employed as a salesman at a car dealership. When business began to increase, the owner hired another salesman. His name was Tony. What Tony may have lacked in sense he certainly made up for in enthusiasm. Tony was out to sell cars by any method that worked.

We each had business cards printed up by the dealership with the automobile dealer's logo. That was not good enough for Tony; he had his own cards printed. They read, "There's no Baloney when you deal with Tony." For the rest of the sales force, we knew that didn't fly; we always put up with 'baloney' with Tony.

Each of us had a new car to drive. Tony had a V-8 Gremlin-X, a hot little model of the early seventies. One morning, Tony came to work, looking like he had not slept all night, and the windows of his car were all shot out! Tony had been getting it on with his upstairs neighbor's wife. The neighbor came home and caught Tony in the act. Enough said. Tony barely escaped with his life. I do not know how he explained this to the owner but his 'baloney' worked. He was given another chance and another demo, this time a Hornet fastback.

In less than a month, Tony's second demo was wrecked. There was a police report that a drunken driver had rammed into him on a north side street in our city. Tony was off the hook for a while. His first demo was repaired, and again he took up the wheel behind the Gremlin-X. The truth finally came out through the grapevine (Tony was pretty free with information); he had been drinking and rammed his Hornet into a steel utility pole. Knowing this would be the end of his sales career, he found a drunk, put him in a car, and convinced him he had been in an accident and wrecked Tony's car. The drunk was there with the wreck when the police arrived.

The owner of the dealership became aware of this incident. Shortly thereafter, Tony was history (or so we thought). Tony did not return, but Tony's 'baloney' was around for quite sometime. A few weeks later, a customer who had purchased a used car from Tony came into the service department with his car. This car was one of those used car specials, no warranty other than 50-50; "after fifty feet or fifty seconds you are on your own." However, when Tony sold a car, he ran his own specials. The customer came in with a hand-written 100 percent warranty, parts and labor, written and signed by Tony. In the next couple of months, we had several of these that the owner had to explain and work through with the customer.

"What were you thinking Tony?" Yes, even Tony was thinking, living for the moment, determined to sell cars, to enjoy pleasures for the moment, not considering the outcome. To himself, he was "no baloney" because he really believed in what he was doing at the very moment of his deeds; whatever works. The end justifies the means. Unfortunately, the ends often proved that his means were somehow faulty.

This story may be an extreme, but it illustrates where we all go sometimes; we get the job done, whatever works. Many of my youthful decisions revolving around relationships were no less faulty. My snap judgment to join the Navy was one of those choices. God taught me many things in the two years I spent aboard ship, but at the time it was very disruptive to my education, family, and relationships.

Although we may not bend the rules and become as devious as Tony, the pressures of our world sometimes move us ahead in decisions that may be full of 'baloney'. Sometimes little thought goes into the choices we make, large and small, even though they may have a bearing on the rest of our lives, and even on our eternity. We continue to live in the labor of life and do not rise above to a higher level of relationship with the God of wisdom.

All persons think. Every action we take requires some level of thinking. We often do not want to admit that thinking went into the process of our choices, especially when there is a bad outcome. We want it to be some uncontrolled reflex action which let's us off the hook. No matter how simple or complex our decisions they begin with 'thinking'.

It is true we may not be aware of more than nine-tenths of our own inner mental activity in the subconscious mind. The psychology of today would like us to believe we have very powerful inner urges that govern our being and prompt us to do many things of which our conscious mind is unaware. We are led to believe that most of the time it is impossible for us to not comply with the commands of that inner power that rules us. There is truth to this, but not because we are simply mechanistic beings, or a chance evolutionary development of the natural order, struggling to ascend from the brutish past. The apostle Paul 's words speak clearly of our inner struggles and identify the cause:

I do not understand what I do. For what I want to do I do not do, but what I hate I do...As it is, it is no longer I myself who do it, but it is sin living in me. [18]I know that nothing good lives in me, that is, in my sinful nature. For I have the desire to do what is good, but I cannot carry it out. For what I do is not the good I want to do; no, the evil I do not want to do—this I keep on doing. [20]Now if I do what I do not want to do, it is no longer I who do it, but it is sin living in me that does it (Romans 7:15,17-20).

It is the sin-nature that clouds our thinking. The secular person in philosophy and science rules out the consideration of sin, because they rule out a supreme being who has established absolute truth. Without a ruler there cannot be a rule.

Many of life's decisions, even life-changing ones, are made with a very superficial thought process. For most, it is just "reflex action" stemming from hurts that have been inflicted, or environmental input over the course of life. Snap judgments and decisions, focusing on simply physical existence and expedient thinking, are evidence that we are not connecting faith and reason.

There is a better way. Thinking can be an intellectual-level process that also includes our very being. The thinking process of history's great thinkers ranges from seeing reality as mechanistic to a more spiritual, metaphysical perspective. Hopefully, the study will encourage each reader to make a decision to become actively involved in the process of thinking, and not just leave it up to powerful urges of an inner ruling force -as Paul would describe it- "the old self."

I believe the thought process that God desires in us involves head and heart. God wants us to come to the place spoken of by the apostle Paul: "Let this mind be in you, which was also in Christ Jesus."[17] Much that is heard today through the medium of television is presented as truth and tugs at the heart. We must involve the heart, but God wants our heart to be guided by the mind. Not a mind filled with the philosophy of the world, but a mind guided by the divine revelation of the Word of God. Paul wrote to the Romans, "Do not conform any longer to the pattern of this world, but be transformed by the renewing of your mind. Then you will be able to test and approve what God's will is—his good, pleasing and perfect will."[18] When we come to the place of understanding His perfect will we are in the place of wisdom; the graduate school of thinking.

Opening the door to heart-level thinking will enable you to honestly look into your own thought process. May this small volume aid in leading you to finding wisdom, the true relationship of faith and reason, and then know that true wisdom is found and totally derived from the Father, and the Lord Jesus Christ, through whom all things came and through whom we live.[19] Without the benefit of a Supreme Being and His authoritative revelation we will continue to live in the fog and confusion that continues to be expressed by the very philosophers who claim to be "lovers of wisdom."

Thinking Questions:

1. How would you define "The stuff of Life?"

2. When we make wrong decisions can God still use us?

3. Discuss the events shared regarding the author's life, and how he responded. Take one event, discuss it and decide how you would have responded?

4. In what ways did the author rely on reason? In what ways did he rely on the heart? Were there situations where he used both heart and head, faith and reason?

5. Consider difficult events in your own life. Do you remember a thinking process as you attempted to deal with those situations?

6. What events in your life have caused you to take inventory of where you are going?

7. What motivated Tony?

8. Is expediency ever the correct decision?

9. Do you struggle with the "old self?"

10. Read Proverbs 3:1-6. How do these verses relate to viewing expediency in your life?

Endnotes

12 "Spilling Over: A Biblical Blueprint for Evangelism." 1977, Bruce Scott Ministries, Box 4000, Station D, Scarborough, Ontario.
13 Romans 8:28
14 2 Corinthians 5:17-19
15 Chapter 1:20,21
16 James 1:5
17 Philippians 2:5
18 Romans 12:2
19 1 Corinthians 8:6

3
Wholeness of Life

The discipline of philosophy in seeking to understand wisdom seems to wander from the path of truth. Philosophers from all ages have sought wisdom through attempting to explain reality or existence. Here are definitions from five philosophers:

- Aristotle believed philosophy was the universal science. He believed all other sciences were branches of philosophy. Aristotle called the study of reality as a whole, "First Philosophy." His idea of philosophy was the interrelation of all knowledge.
- Bertrand Russell and Hans Rechenback taught that philosophy equals logic. They restricted it to methodology, not unlike secular scientists of our modern world.
- Matthew Arnold defined philosophy as "seeing life steadily and seeing it whole."
- Edgar S. Brightman defined it as "The coherent view of life," similar to Arnold's view.
- Warren C. young wrote, "Man is a creature of many and varied experiences. Each experience by itself is but a fragment- a piece in the jigsaw puzzle of life. No piece may be left out if the picture is to be complete. To philosophize is simply to try to integrate one's life experiences."[20]

All the definitions share the idea of wholeness or integration of life experiences, except Russell's. His restriction of philosophy to methods is no different than the laborer who sees life as simply the sum of his or her

25

physical labors. The "methodist" (no denominational pun intended) is often found in the seat of higher learning doling out "wisdom" by trying to methodically or mechanically organize everything. The assumption is made that somehow out of order comes meaning. This *order* may also be a sign of insecurities. Attempting to control everything is evidence of an inward struggle to know an abiding purpose. Although we have great evidence of the orderliness of God in creation, understanding order alone will not lead to wisdom.

"Order" is sometimes confused with the godly life. Conservative Christianity sometimes lapses into a similar philosophy like the legalistic Pharisees of the first century, by attempting to put all belief into a logical order (according to a particular theological structure) and then proclaiming that order as the gospel. All those who accept the ordered teachings are in the fold; those who do not are considered ungodly persons.

"Order" for some means crossing every "T" and dotting every "I" of Scripture, without practical application. In the sixties, a popular phrase among seminarians was "bibliolatry." The term implied worshipping the Scripture as an idol. The Bible reveals God to us so we might know Him and worship and serve Him; religious study of the Scripture without application can become idolatrous. Jesus said, "...go and make disciples of all nations, ...teaching them to obey everything I have commanded you."[21] Teaching and preaching was to be carried out for the purpose of obedience; living out God's truth in our lives.

During a "Walk Through the Bible" seminar, Bruce Wilkinson shared his journey from the land of "order" to spiritual application. He identified the revelations that transformed his preaching. He began to look closely at the preaching and teaching of Christ. Wilkinson realized it was 98 percent application. He also learned that most great bible teachers and evangelists during times of spiritual awakening and renewal were teaching and preaching application of the Word. He identified that John Wesley, the one who almost single-handedly transformed England in the 18th century, was preaching a 98 percent application of the gospel. Wilkinson's seminary training had prepared him to have the traditional three-point outline of the subject, with a quick, application to tie it up in a nice neat package and bring closure.

Once he was aware of the place of application, his ministry began to see spiritual multiplication.

One professor in graduate school was caught up in the "school of order," the three-point life. His teaching method was very rigid, accepting no questioning from his students. During his lectures on the Hebrew of the Old Testament, students suspected that his detailed analysis of Scripture served no purpose other than to know as the Pharisees did, every "jot and tittle" of the books. One very brilliant fellow classman set a verbal trap for the professor. As the class lecture continued, with several well-phrased questions from students, it suddenly dawned on the professor that his words had found him out; he had no higher goal for us than to know the Scripture for the sake of knowing Scripture. There were no deeper spiritual intentions. The mask had been subtly ripped away. His image suddenly turned from the stern but gentle college professor to a red-faced, angry visage. He abruptly ended his lecture and dismissed the class. Never again, did he allow the discussion to go there. Order alone does not lead to wisdom.

A more humorous incident in graduate school illustrates the proper place of order. While I was a student at Wheaton Graduate School in 1966, I had the privilege of sitting under the disciplined but in-depth tutelage of Dr. J. Barton Payne, in Old Testament studies. For each class day we were given assigned book readings from volumes on reserve in the graduate school library. The building was situated on the opposite corner from Buswell Hall, the graduate building. Every day like clockwork, Dr. Payne would appear from across the street near "The Stupe" (the campus sandwich/soda shop), walking with perfectly measured steps to the sidewalk in front of Buswell. He would set down his briefcase without losing his stride and continue on to the library to gather up the reserved books for the day's assignment. On his return, armed with books, he would reach down and pick up his briefcase with out glancing down or breaking his measured cadence. Dr. Payne would then enter the building and our classroom, ready to begin class, with an incredible energy and enthusiasm that was his trademark.

Daily watching this scenario from the windows of the graduate building classroom initiated a mischievous plot in the devious minds of grad students (apparently without much excitement in our lives). We were convinced Dr. Payne recorded in his mind the exact number of steps, to and from the Library, that it took to arrive back at the exact spot where he so trustingly had deposited his briefcase. What if, he arrived back to the spot and the briefcase was gone?

One afternoon, seeing the familiar scene take place, we rushed out, retrieved his briefcase and placed it on his desk. Then we watched with anticipation from the window. He did not disappoint us. Leaving the library, and approaching the briefcase with his very familiar pace, he reached down at the exact location, and appeared to almost stumble, because his hand did not grasp the familiar handle. He stood up, with hand on his chin, rolled his eyes with a growing look of awareness, rolling his tongue in his cheek in a look that only those who knew him could describe. Dr. Payne continued on inside the building and into the classroom full of seated chessy-cat looking students. Now wearing a very mischievous look and dancing eyes, he asked if anyone had possibly seen his missing briefcase.

Probably reflecting the lack of wisdom on our part, a few days later we repeated this trick. Much to our surprise after the second attempt, he did not reprimand or become angry with his immature students. Rather, in spite of what seemed to be a regulated, rigid pattern of our professor that could not be changed, Dr. Payne never again left his briefcase on the sidewalk, but continued on to the library, carrying it and returning with books and case in a new, very strident manner.

How does this incident speak of wisdom in relationship to order? It is a very simple, yet profound truth: Dr. Payne's precise, organized life was not ordered so as to find wisdom; his detailed systematic lifestyle grew out of his wisdom and understanding of his faith in the God of order. He knew his Lord intimately and lived out his life applying God's truths, in a uniquely ordered manner as a servant so that he would not waste any precious moment of his life. His response and example to his mischievous students was not that of an unbending, unchangeable person; but a deeply committed Christian whose personal details were neither immutable or his "stuff of life."

A later incident, when I had returned to campus to defend my thesis illustrates this gracious professor's true order of life. A friend, named Read, was attending the "ordered," lockstep seminary where I had enrolled, in Michigan. He was looking for a school where he could pursue a master's in communication, and have more freedom of choices. I recommended that he go with me when I returned to Wheaton. When we arrived on campus, it was exam time; professors were up to their ears in grading and correcting tests and term papers, and Dr. Payne was no exception. I went to Dr. Payne's office with Reed, walked in and introduced him. Dr. Payne, in the midst of his workload, with carefully arranged piles on his desk, rolled back his chair turned to Read, talking with him for over an hour, as if there was nothing more important in the world at that moment. The proof, as they say, is in the pudding. Read transferred and later graduated from Wheaton.

Is there a parallel here? I believe so, without stretching too far. We can live an ordered life that is not unchangeable, and be personable and relational. This is a good illustration of faith and reason. For many, faith is understood as feeling and to arrive there it is necessary to jump off the solid rocks of reason into the murky, unknown waters of faith. Christians, of almost all ages, have spoken regarding "the blind leap of faith." Faith does not lead us away from reason; faith enables us to reason and cut through the age-old confusion of mankind brought about by the sinful nature. We can sit at the professor desk of ordered rational thought and by faith understand the relational aspects of life and reach out to others. We can reach out, not unbending, but understanding that the very created order of a sovereign God frees us to be flexible, creative, caring, growing, and "seeing life whole" persons.

Does a philosophy that embraces the whole range of human experience give us a complete and whole view of life? Does it answer the unspoken questions we all ask? The previous definitions ignore one essential aspect. It is necessary to have someone exterior to our experience that is capable of viewing accurately all of human experiences in one great, united panorama. No one but God has that viewpoint. Without this view, it is impossible to have correct thinking.

I remember an old cartoon that illustrates this idea. A small fellow was wandering through a forest of trees. He stops to rest, leaning against what he believes to be a tree trunk. Suddenly the tree moves. It turns out to be the legs of a large elephant standing in the midst of the trees. The surroundings were all trees from this man's perspective. The view in the cartoon, however, shows the trees, the man, and the elephant rising above the trees. Someone must have that panoramic view of life.

All of us have a "world and life view" although we may not recite it or be aware of it. The world and life view that we hold will be the philosophy by which we will "make" or "not make decisively" all our decisions. Our world and life view will determine our thinking process. No individual can possibly view in his lifetime all of human experience. We often lean on elephant legs because of our limited experience. There is one "world and life" view that addresses this limitation of the human spirit: the revelation of God through the Scriptures. To have a complete and coherent view of life we must rely on the one who can see above the forest; who not only sees the elephant but also created him.

Thinking Questions

1. Write your own definition of philosophy.

2. Discuss the confusion of "order" with "godliness."

3. Are you able to articulate your world and life view?

4. Why do some persons seek order in their lives while some appear to hunt for every means to live in chaos?

5. What place does "order" hold in your understanding of life?

6. What place does "order" hold in an understanding of faith?

7. What was the fundamental difference between the two professors' views of order?

8. In your experience has organized religion focused on order to the exclusion of relationship?

9. Is it possible to "see life whole" without divine guidance?

10. Read Job 38 and 39. What is the admonition that God is giving to Job?

11. Consider areas in your life where you may be leaning on "elephant legs."

Endnotes

[20] Warren C. Young, "A Christian Approach to Philosophy," Baker Book House, Grand Rapids, 1962. p. 22.

[21] Matthew 28:19,20

4
Branches of the Tree

Don't be frightened or intimidated as we "branch out" into philosophy. When we understand the branches they can become our friends. It is important to know these disciplines for they can help us in our thinking process. Many writers and teachers in our modern world misuse them.

1. **Methodology:** This comes from the Greek word meaning "to trace, investigate, to handle methodically, or to handle cunningly. This is the toolbox of philosophers (This is also the meeting place of science and philosophy. In many cases both use the same toolbox).

2. **Epistemology:** This comes from a combination of the Greek words "knowledge" and "word." This discipline deals with the methods and basis of knowledge. This discipline deals with the limits and validity of knowledge. It is a lack in understanding this discipline that opens the door to many accepting fictional writings such as "The Da Vinci Code" as fact, or putting the recently examined "Gospel of Judas" on a par with Scripture.

3. **Metaphysics:** This word comes from the French and the Greek words "after" and "physic" or "physical." The latter word means "natural." So metaphysics is the discipline that studies that which is "beyond nature." The traditional divisions of metaphysics are:

a. Ontology: nature of being
b. Cosmology: nature of the World.
c. Psychology: nature of the soul.
d. Theology: nature of God
   We can study metaphysics in the Bible; Genesis, the "book of beginnings," is a basis for this discipline. Regrettably, in this age of specialization and mechanization, the traditional divisions of metaphysics are often considered obsolete.

4. **Axiology:** This word comes from the Greek, which means "worthy of study." This is the theory and study of values, primarily of intrinsic values, as those in ethics, aesthetics, and religion (the good, the beautiful, the holy). It is also a study of instrumental values such as those within the discipline of economics. The subdivisions are:
   a. Ethics: concerned with human behavior both individually and socially. Ethics is concerned not with the actual, but what ought to be, the ideal.
   b. Aesthetics: This is concerned with humanity's sense of beauty.
   c. Philosophy of History: Study concerned with whether there is a guiding principle or a directive purpose in history.

Relation of philosophy to the sciences

Philosophy attempts to relate and integrate all the information from the different fields of science. The following chart identifies the terms associated with philosophy and those terms associated with science.

Science-	Philosophy-
Deals with analysis	Deals with synopsis
Deals with the discovery and investigation of factual data	Deals with the meaning and significance of data
Deals with discovery	Deals with interpretation

Deals with revealing of facts

Deals with relation and integration of facts

The relationship of these respective terms to philosophy and science is very important. In today's postmodern world, science (sometimes "falsely so-called") tries to assume the role of the philosopher, assuming the Bertrand Russell approach that methodology alone can be a complete integration and presentation of all of life's experiences. This "scientific" approach recognizes only the material world.

The Greek thinkers

Let us look a little more in depth at three of the Greek philosophers and their contribution to man's quest for wisdom. One of the greatest achievements and contributions of the Greeks was in the area of philosophy. The Greek philosophers of the fourth and fifth centuries B.C. were interested not only in attempting to explain the universe, but also in the ethical and moral problems of humanity. They sought to find a perfect form of life.

Socrates wrote nothing. For this reason many parallels have been drawn between Socrates and Christ. The only evidence we have of Christ writing was in the dust, as he confronted the accusers of the woman who committed adultery.[22] In the same manner that we learn of Christ through the writings of his disciples, we only know Socrates teaching through the writings of Plato and other disciples. Socrates did not lecture, but asked questions, demonstrated the false logic in the answer, then asked more questions. Socrates set a higher ethical standard (except Jesus) than any of the philosophers. This was his greatest contribution.

Plato was a student of Socrates. His own philosophy both altered and added to those of his teacher. Plato's writings were in the form of dialogues, like those conducted by Socrates. Plato sought to find out the eternally valid universal forms, of which individual actions or things are but imperfect expressions. He believed his so-called "universal ideas" could be used to discover the rational order existing in the world.[23]

35

Aristotle's philosophy covered a much greater range of subject matter than Plato's. Aristotle was concerned with the natural sciences and with factual knowledge of the universe. He was also a student of Biology, which made him more aware of the constant process of change in the natural order.

Aristotle's form of writing favored a simple scientific process. His work included studies in many fields: Physics, Astronomy, Biology, Psychology, Metaphysics, Logic (deductive reasoning), Ethics, Politics, Theory of Rhetoric, and Poetry. Although wrong in some of his reasoning because of false premises, Aristotle was still a genius of his day. He laid the groundwork for much of modern day studies. Dante called him, "The master of those who know."

My First Impressions of this "Stuff of Wisdom."

In undergraduate days, I was asked to give my first impression of philosophy, implying the class work just completed had been my first encounter. I attempted to answer the question by relating my earlier personal life experiences. My answer was an endeavor to focus on the first period of my life when I became aware that this thought process of integration was taking place. I recounted my first remembrances of grappling with the stuff of philosophy. As I have already shared, I had numerous difficult incidents in my life that caused me to consider whether or not God had a plan for my life. I believe I first began the process of integrating those experiences when I was called to active duty in the Navy.

I spent two years in 13 countries of the world, traveling on a "cruise ship" (the USS Essex CVA-9). The Essex was a 40,000, ton displacement aircraft carrier, 900 feet long. It was a floating city, dubbed, "The 'Fightinist' Ship in the Fleet." At this crossroads of life, having completed high school, 1-1/2 years of college, three or four romances and planning marriage; having experienced salvation, separation from loved ones, world travel, customs of other countries, other peoples, and terrible loneliness, my first impression of philosophy was just shy of complete confusion.

I did not accept my new circumstances meekly; for weeks, crossing the Atlantic Ocean, traveling farther and farther from loved ones, I was angry with God. I had a desk in Primary Fly (the air control tower aboard carriers), and on that desk I had a bible. Often, at night, before we began flights, I would walk up and down in front of that desk, alone in the tower, having a debate with God over opening the Bible and reading it. I did not want to let go of my hurt and loneliness even though I knew I would find answers in Scripture. After all, it was God's fault! One night, His persistent grace finally pierced my heart. I sat down, in the red glow of the night-light, and opened the book. The Bible fell open to what has become my life verse, which I read and re-read that night with tears dripping on the pages:

> If the LORD delights in a man's way, he makes his steps firm; though he stumble, he will not fall, for the LORD upholds him with his hand.[24]

I certainly had stumbled often, and sometimes fell on my face. Dimly, I began to realize all experiences, both glad and sad, must have a purpose. The light was beginning to dawn that in order to gather my life together and direct it towards that purpose I must rely on divine guidance, or continue to lean on elephant legs.

Relating Biblical Study to Philosophy

Paul wrote to Timothy, his spiritual son, "Do your best to present yourself to God as one approved, a workman who does not need to be ashamed and who correctly handles the word of truth."[25] He earlier had written to him these words: "Timothy, guard what has been entrusted to your care. Turn away from godless chatter and the opposing ideas of what is falsely called knowledge, which some have professed and in so doing have wandered from the faith."[26] As his spiritual father, Paul had committed to Timothy the work of ministry, proclaiming the Gospel of Jesus Christ. I too, was called to the ministry. In one sense, all who profess faith in Jesus Christ are called to minister. Perhaps not to pastor or to pursue a mission field, but wherever God places us, we are to be His witness. Under the marching orders of this great commission, I accepted the Scripture as the authoritative Word of God. I believe it to be inspired, and that it alone is a Christian's standard of faith and practice. I determine not to conform the Bible to any philosophy, but to be a person who "correctly handles the word of truth" using it to measure the worth of any teaching.

The saddest experience in my journey of faith has been the observance that many Christian leaders allow a system of theology or doctrinal beliefs to be a sifting grid to study scripture. Instead of developing their theology from the Bible. Scripture rests on the shaky foundation of their theological framework. It is important to know and understand how to approach Scripture. There are few evangelical Christians who would disagree on the methods of interpreting the Bible. Unfortunately, lacking the understanding of a proper thought process, there are many who have not been faithful to those methods.

Cyrus Scofield's little book "Rightly Dividing the Word of Truth" is the perfect example of not allowing the Scripture to be foundational. Scofield's book used the King James translation of 1 Timothy 2:15: "Study to show thyself approved unto God, a workman that needeth not to be ashamed, *rightly dividing* the word of truth." "The phrase in the scriptural context refers to the right handling of Scripture, as translated in the NIV: "Do your best to present yourself to God as one approved, a workman who does not need to be ashamed and who *correctly handles* the word of truth." It does not refer to cutting up the Bible for different purposes and persons. Yet, Scofield used this well-known phrase from the letter to Timothy to support dividing scripture, arbitrarily assigning certain portions to Israel and other portions to the Church, literally proclaiming three of the gospels, containing much of our Lord's teaching, as meant only for Israel. The phrase has been misused to wrest away the words of our Savior from God's true people, the Church, and give them to the "adulterous generation of Israel" after the flesh. The very words from Paul given for the purpose of mentoring Timothy his spiritual son in correct handling of truth have been used to distort the singularity of the Gospel for all persons, whether Jew or any other nationality.[27]

The Christian should be familiar with two areas of philosophy: those philosophies current during the lifetime of the writers of scripture and contemporary philosophies in our present day. Knowing the teachings current during the time of Biblical writers will help us to better understand the scriptural refutations, see clearly the environmental conditions in the time when they lived, and recognize those forces which were influencing their lives.

By knowing the philosophies of our postmodern world, we will be better able to interact with persons of our world, and recognize the shades of gray teachings so embedded in the fabric of our lives. This knowledge will aid us in keeping that truth that is committed to our trust, avoid profane and vain babblings, rightly handle the Word of truth, and establish a world and life view consistent with the Word of God.

Sadly, the focus of today's education does not lead to objective understanding of truth. Allan Bloom, the late professor at University of Chicago in the area of social thought, authored the book, "The Closing of the American Mind." "What we see today, according to Bloom, is young people who, lacking an understanding of the past and a vision of the future, live in an impoverished present."[28] That impoverishment has affected an entire generation and leads only to a confused thought process. Evaluate your thinking today. Does it rest on the shaky fabric of our nonsensical culture, or does it find its foundation in the eternal proven teachings of the God of truth?

Thinking Questions

1. In your own words, describe the difference between philosophy and science.

2. Should science, which is basically an investigative process of physical data, assume the role of philosophy and attempt to be an integrator of life's experiences?

3. Which one of the Greek thinkers can you identify with?

4. What is the "stuff of wisdom" in your life experiences?

5. Do you believe you allow the Scripture to guide you, or is it a system of belief you have been taught?

6. What constant principle exists that would be the same for both first century philosophy and the twenty-first century?

7. Read 2 Timothy 2:14-26. Discuss the "stuff of wisdom" that Paul shares with Timothy. Consider in what ways you can apply these verses to your own life experiences.

Endnotes

22 John 8:11
23 Young, loc. Cit., p.23
24 Psalm 37:23,24
25 2 Timothy 2:15 (KJV)
26 1 Timothy 6:20
27 For further study regarding this aberration of the Gospel, refer to "Beyond Da Vinci: The True Bride of Christ" by J. Ingram.
28 Simon and Schuster, New york, 1987, dustjacket.

5
Don't assume too much

In this chapter we want to deal with the problem of assumptions. To do so, we must look at four areas: methodology, the relationship of faith and reason, relation of assumptions to world and life views, and a deeper look at the scientific method.

Methodology is comprised of the logic and presuppositions of the various philosophers. For the most part, methods of man rely on observation and reasoning. Observation and reasoning are further sub-divided into various classifications of methods. A philosopher does not just sit and think in a daydream fashion, as the well-known sculpture by Auguste Rodin seems to represent. There is some process by which they reason and arrive at conclusions. We are going to explore these methods.

The Rational or Deductive Method

Deduction is the process of reasoning from the *general* to the *specific*—reasoning from general claims that the thinker already knows to a specific conclusion. This method credits man with the ability to discover truth through his own intellectual capacity, without the help of any exterior evidence received through the senses. Plato believed man is born with innate knowledge. Plato considered the evidence received through sense experience was only opinion, but that it helped in recalling the inward, instinctive knowledge. Some strong-willed adolescents evidence this idea in their approach to life. This can be a great limitation to the learning process. It is also contrary to the belief that understanding of truth can only come through reception of God's spirit.

Aristotle continued developing the deductive method. He wrote the laws of deduction as he perceived them. Today's deductive or formal logic classes still follow his pattern. Plato considered the physical world of senses merely an illusion, while Aristotle believed the place of thinking is found first in the realm of the physical world.[29]

Experimental or Inductive Method

This method is widely accepted. This is reasoning proceeding from *particular* facts to a *general* conclusion The inductive method is often called the empirical, scientific, or laboratory method.[30] Analysis is one form of the experimental or inductive method. This tool of discovery came into use in the time of Francis Bacon, in the 1600's. Bacon attempted to express the spirit of the age in his *Novum Organum* (1620). He introduced this work as inductive logic in contrast with deductive reasoning, which Aristotle developed, and which Bacon believed the Church was using to support its teachings.[31]

The essential of the inductive method of study are:
1. Investigation or gathering data.
2. Organization or arranging data.
3. Hypothesis, suggestion of a tentative solution.
4. Verification, or rejection of the hypothesis.

Romantic Method

This method is based on feelings and instincts. For anyone who has been in love this method requires no definition. The method was adopted to fight extreme rationalism in philosophy and theology. Many in today's church tend to lean towards feelings and emotions, rather than an in-depth and rational study of the Scripture.

Dialectical Method

Dialectic is formal logical argument. The dialectical method is a way of extending reason to its absolute limits and discovering that its limits extend much farther than one would have ever imagined. This method using debate and argumentation is probably one of the oldest processes of philosophy. Socrates employed this method and in modern times, Soren Kierkegaard began a form of the dialectical method among theologians.

Synoptic Method

The synoptic method is a summary or general view of the whole. Proponents of this method believe a coherent view of life can only be found if you leave nothing out. In other words, if a philosophy of life is to be of any value, "it must embrace the whole range of human experience."[32] There is sound logic in this view. However, we must ask, "Whose experience encompasses the whole range of human experience?"

Descartes' Method of Doubt

Entering into every human life is the element of doubt. It is certainly a part of the human experience with which we must deal. Many in today's society are skeptics, and some magazine publications are dedicated to skepticism. Descartes, a Frenchman, developed his philosophy because of dissatisfaction with the Roman Catholic Church. Growing out of that discontent he began his search with doubt. His beginning hypothesis was the assertion of universal doubt. This statement sums up his philosophy: "Anything not positively proved could be in error." Descartes developed three principles:

1. The truth of his own existence. "I think, therefore, I am."
2. The truth of God's existence. He felt the presence in his mind of the idea of an infinite being was proof of that being's existence. He believed that since he was a finite being, to conceive of an infinite being was proof that it was true.
3. The truth of the existence of the created order. Arguing from the basis of his second truth, he believed that his perceptions of the world had to be true since the infinite God would not deceive.

The major fallacy of his philosophy was assuming an *idea* was synonymous with the object of the *idea*. "I think, therefore I am." When in a deep sleep we do not know whether we are thinking or not. When we wake up we may remember a dream or two but when we think about it that may only add up to about five minutes in length even though we know we were asleep for eight hours. There is all of that time when we don't remember what we were thinking or if we were even thinking at all. Descartes would argue that even if we do not remember we are always thinking, for to not think would mean we do not exist.

Contrary to Descartes' belief, our mind is capable of ideas that may have no existence in reality. Individuals who struggle with God having foreknowledge are subconsciously making this assumption. Their argument goes something like this: "God knows the choice in His mind therefore He is making the choice, so I cannot have free will." God's foreknowledge of our choices in the future makes them no less our choices. What it does say of God is he is giving us *freedom* of choice because in spite of foreknowledge, He does not block our wrong decisions.

Descartes philosophy was published in his "Discourse on Method" in 1637, his "Meditations" in 1641, and in "Principles of Philosophy" in 1644. Further study carried Descartes into the interaction of spirit and matter. Amazingly, Descartes was led to this belief: the interaction of spirit and matter was a miracle that happened because of the omnipotence of God.[33]

Induction

Induction can be defined as "the process of drawing a general conclusion from particular facts."[34] John Stuart Mill (1806-1873) first formulated the laws of induction in his work, "System of Logic (1843). Induction is comprised of four main essentials:

1. Investigation or gathering data
2. Organization of data.
3. Hypothesis of data.
4. Verification.

Mill's logic was an attempt to formulate an understanding of how persons actually make inferences from one set of particular facts to another set of facts.[35]   He believed that unexplained events must be traced to new causes.[36]

Hegel's Method

Hegel's method stems from the method of debate and argumentation, the dialectical method. He developed a dialectical triad:

1. Thesis is the start of any point in experience.
2. Antithesis is the point to which the mind moves in thought, anywhere other than the starting point.
3. Synthesis is the opposition growing from the first two; it brings the thinker to something new or different. This process is

continually repeated. The highest synthesis possible is believed to be absolute spirit.

The Relationship of Faith and Reason

"How will I relate faith and reason in the problems and decisions that I will face today?" I am sure most of us do not begin each day and verbalize this thinking to ourselves. Yet it is a way that we struggle with the day-to-day routines especially if we have faith and want to please God in all that we do. There are five relationships between faith and reason. The philosophers thought about these relationships and attempted to define them. Knowingly or unknowingly we connect our personal faith with our rationale in one of these ways.

1. **Faith precedes reason.** Some theologians who held this view are Calvin and Cornelius Van Til.
2. **Faith transcends reason.** This view states that scientific reason is based on faith. Thomas Aquinas held this view.
3. **Mutual dependence of faith and reason.** The two are hand in hand and cannot be separated. Tertullian (160-220 a.d.) held to this view.
4. **Reason is supreme.** This is called "Rationalism." Man has rational powers that unaided by God can arrive at truth. Much of the scientific world has moved beyond science as the discipline of discovery to a rationalistic faith that believes science alone can arrive at all truth. Extra-sensory or metaphysical aspects of life are ignored or their existence denied.
5. **Faith is supreme.** This was the view of Pascal (1623-1662). God exists to be experienced, not to be rationalized. This is the basic understanding in Christian mysticism. Many who claim to be religious or persons of faith in today's world, having accepted the extended claims of scientific philosophy as truth, place faith in this unstable vessel of mystic religion.

There is one additional theory, held by Kant (1724-1804). Kant's theory divorces faith and reason. He believed that knowledge must be restricted to the realm of the physical world and that all human knowledge is furnished by the senses. In Kant's "Critique of Practical Reason" he tries to show that it is reasonable to believe in the supernatural (God). This belief requires faith, which Kant describes as *practical reason*. This comes about through the individual's logical arguments. This "faith" does not seem to bear any relationship to the definition of faith as found in the Scriptures.

I do not believe that Kant's "divorce is possible. There are those, however, who have been proponents of the other extreme: a very close relationship of faith and reason that also does not appear to support biblical faith. Some who have held this position are Brightman (1884-1953), Ferre' (1933-), Ramsdell (1895-1939), and Machen (1881-1937). Their association of faith and reason appears to be no more than a complex view of reason alone. There is a very interesting quote of Edgar Brightman which sums up this view: "If there is a God, man's immortality is certain. If not, Immortality would not be worth having."

I believe that faith and reason must not be separated, but faith precedes reason. Faith apart from reason may be no faith at all, or it may be faith in that which is not true. Augustine (354-430 a.d.) said, "We believe in order to understand." If we do not express a certain fundamental faith I believe it is impossible to understand anything. Faith is necessary to all knowing. Faith is the basic category of all human existence. However, true faith is an element that is lacking in the existence of a majority of the populace. Nervousness, anxiety, and extreme depression, are not symptoms of a *loss* of faith but a *lack* of it.

I would like to use three illustrations that may help us to see this view of faith. First, I have often heard ministers use the illustration of sitting in a chair to illustrate faith. We sit in the chair without forethought; we have perfect faith that it will hold us. Faith in Christ is described in this fashion. "Don't worry, just have faith." Yet is this a true illustration of believing faith? I do not believe that the "faith" it takes to sit in a chair aptly illustrates faith in God. It falls into the category of reason alone.

1. We have sat in chairs enumerable times before and we have seen others sit in chairs. There does not seem to be any active

thought process outside of human habit at work in the act of sitting.

2. The chair is sitting on solid ground. If it collapsed, for most persons it would not allow a fall far enough to hurt us.
3. I do not need faith in this act of sitting. It is neither complex nor dangerous and in no way affects my peace of mind.

For the second illustration, let's leave the usual, calm situation of our daily lives and consider an unusual, dangerous one. A person is in a life raft adrift on a vast ocean. The waves are high; there are terrible winds and stormy conditions. In this situation, it would appear that reason is useless, except in small ways that might be considered to keep the raft from capsizing. Faith must enter into this equation.

1. The raft is unstable; it could be punctured.
2. It is not on a solid foundation. If the person loses this platform under the circumstances, it would mean death.
3. Reason cannot give this man any assurance of safety or peace of mind. It would take faith to have any serenity.

For the third illustration, let us go to Niagara Falls. In years past there were many daredevils conducting dangerous thrills to challenge the power and danger of the Falls. Many have attempted to go over the Falls in a barrel. Most lost their lives. Below the falls where the gorge narrows, there is a bend in the river that creates a whirlpool effect in the raging waters. Many years ago, a tightrope walker maneuvered a wheelbarrow across the gorge on a rope. He would invite someone to join him in the wheelbarrow. Two persons were watching this feat from the rim of the gorge. We'll call them Jim and Joan. Jim said to Joan, "Do you see that incredible feat, Joan?" Joan replies, "Of course I see it!" "Do you think I am blind?" Jim continues, "Do you really believe it, Joan?" Joan replies, "Of course I believe it!" "I see it with my own eyes!" Then Jim drives home his point: "Well then, since you believe it, will you get in the wheel-barrow and let him take you across?" Joan emphatically replied, "No!" "It will never happen!"

1. Joan saw the event, she perceived of it through her senses.
2. Joan believed the event was happening through her senses.

3. Joan did not have the faith to trust the man and get in the wheelbarrow.

Whatever view we hold of the account of creation in Genesis, we must recognize in the story God's incredible wisdom in depicting faith and reason in terms of the Tree of Life and the Tree of the Knowledge of Good and Evil. In the New Testament, life in the spirit is depicted as "fruit of the Spirit."[37]   Fruit has seeds.   God wanted mankind to nurture the spirit life of faith, not the seeds of knowledge apart from faith.   The earliest distortion of a right relationship with God by Satan was Gnosticism; through knowledge mankind would be like God and have life (Gnosticism is still alive and well in such publications as "The Da Vinci Code).   Mankind had access to the Tree of Life as long as they trusted and served the Creator.   Unfortunately, Adam and Eve failed the test of faith and sought the fruit of the knowledge of Good and Evil, believing there was more to life than a perfect relationship with the creator.

God does not withhold wisdom and knowledge from us; He desires that we have it. He does not want us to seek knowledge apart from Him or apart from a spiritual understanding; that will only lead to confusion and death. We are not to divorce faith and reason, which was the first great divorce of history, the wrong choices in Eden.

Nervousness, anxieties, depressions, worry, are symptoms of not having faith. We look to reason for our answers to carry us through life. Faith in ourselves is not faith; it is nothing more than human reason. When the complexities in the sea of life become too great for the feeble bark of reason, man becomes frustrated. Reason sees and believes from the physical evidence the wheelbarrow is real and can carry a person across the gorge. Reason cannot meet the situation and guarantee peace of mind. Faith says to reason, "Will you get in the wheel-barrow?" Reason answers with and emphatic "NO!" Reason and faith must connect to complete the journey.

John R. Ingram

The Importance of Assumptions

Every person has a system of thought by which they live. Sometimes this is called a "World and life view." Some may believe their system is a coherent view of life, while others may not consciously recognize their thought process. Recognition of the process that guides our everyday decision-making is woefully lacking in both Christian lives and secular lifestyles. In this ever-changing world of discovery we need to understand our world and life view and believe in something real in order to survive.

Our world and life views, whether consciously recognized or not, are based on assumptions. These assumptions may or may not be accurate, which will impact how we view life and whether on not we view it in a wholesome fashion. Yet assumptions are necessary to relate and integrate our experiences of life. In many observations, it would appear that the scientifically oriented person of the modern world is comfortable with the assumptions made in science; they have faith in those assumptions. Yet, when it comes to spiritual faith, they stumble over any leap of faith or assumptions regarding Scripture in spite of the immense number of demonstrable historical proofs.

Relationship of assumptions to a philosophy of life

Philosophical assumptions may be divided into four main categories: Rationalism, Naturalism (modern day's scientific method), Idealism, and Christian Realism.

Advocates of **Rationalism** were Descartes (1596-1650), Spinoza (1632-1677), and Socrates (469-399 a.d.). They believed in the construction of a system after the form of mathematics or geometry built on pure reason. Their view was knowledge is innate and only needed development to understand it.

Rationalism is not a recent idea and has been more or less rejected by present philosophers. There have been recent trends that seem to be a new emergence of this viewpoint. A recent TV show called "Numbers" represents a mathematician employed by the FBI to solve crimes based on complex mathematical assumptions.

Naturalists all agree that the scientific method is the only way to obtain truth. This method is understood as it is applied to a particular area of study. Since the sciences are so numerous, so the methods are numerous. True science does not attempt to study all of reality. Science studies a portion of the whole. It does not explain data; it only discovers it. The true scientist recognizes the scientific method as a tool of evidence gathering and discovery. The steps are simple:

1. Research – collecting information and data
2. Question – What is the problem to be solved?
3. Hypothesis – An assumption of what you believe your research will support
4. Project experimentation – testing your hypothesis
5. Conclusion – what the testing has proven relative to the hypothesis

The area of study will flavor the naturalist's conclusions when attempt is made to use a particular method. The naturalist cannot attempt to study the whole of reality. True Science can only be applied to the realm of sense perception, which eliminates the inclusion of the supernatural. Naturalists want to make this method supreme and to include all of existence. They in effect, make the method god-like, supreme above all other philosophies or methods of arriving at truth.

The theory of evolution is an example of an attempt to go beyond the bounds of the scientific method and apply assumptions to theoretical data, which has no basis in fact. Although the naturalist does not believe in faith, they take a giant "leap of faith" to build on theoretical assumptions a complete view of origins outside the realm of scientific discovery. A recent media presentation of the space satellite in orbit around Saturn revealed the "religious fervor" of scientists who continually seek to find an earth-like moon or planet like our own where they might find the process of "spontaneous generation" of life from non-living entities. While continuing to search for the illusive evidence of a mechanistic beginning of life, they boldly support their theory of origins as fact.

Idealists strive to systematically develop a rational system to study the whole of reality. This is a form of Empiricism, but it is not limited to sense experience. The idealist examines experiences to determine if they are coherent and valid. The criteria of coherency are the idealist's personal set of standards. This is the fallacy in this system. Their conclusions are not facts, but probabilities.

The idealists' experimental method applies to the whole realm of reality. The method is only as valid as the personal evaluation of the experiences. For every idealist evaluating the experiences there could be a different set of conclusions. This method of assumptions would seem to lead us to an incoherent system with no valid norm of truth.

The **Christian realist's** basic assumption is belief in the supernatural. To arrive at truth, a fully coherent world and life view, we must go beyond the natural and receive our standard of coherency from one who is beyond our realm of perception – the supernatural God. In God we find the one who is able to view all of reality as a whole and reveal truth.

For the Christian realist, realism is God, and a true revelation of His truth is found in the Scriptures, His divine communication to mankind. God's standard of truth can be applied to all of reality; the assumptions are found to be consistent in every science, in every experience and in every individual mind. As in all systems of thought, Christian realism still requires an assumption. The witness of faith accepts the assumption as truth. The only pre-requisite assumption for the Christian realist is "In the beginning God..." who then reveals Himself to the person of faith.

Positivism

"Positivism" is the name for (at least) two philosophical directions. They have in common the idea of a science without theology or metaphysics, based only on facts about the physical, material world. Structural anthropologist Edmund Leach described *positivism* during the 1966 Henry Myers Lecture:

Positivism is the view that serious scientific inquiry should not search for ultimate causes deriving from some outside source but must confine itself to the study of relations existing between facts which are directly accessible to observation.

"How do we know what we know?" "What is the basis for arriving at truth?" The empiricist, using the scientific method, would say the five senses allow man to understand and enjoy the world. The question is this: Is it possible to evaluate the whole person by scientific means apart from any intangible qualities or values such as love, sacrifice or honesty? Some supporters of this method are Heraclites (circa 500 b.c.), John Locke (1632-1704), Berkeley (1685-1753), and Hume (1711-1776). This form of the scientific method originated in Empiricism. The basic tenets are-

1. The quantitative method, which is relative and changing, is the only method of knowing truth.
2. Man is a creature of only *one* environment.
3. True knowledge is to be obedient to nature, the natural law.
4. Only science can break through to reality's structure.
5. Philosophy is only useful to clarify terms and sentences. Only statements that define mechanistic operations are factual.
6. Only factual propositions that can be quantitatively measured terminate in reality.
7. Philosophy must be precise, objective and unambiguous.
8. Non-cognitive (extra-sensory) meanings have emotional value only. They have no informative or factual function.

This method completely discards the Christian Realist argument, disregarding the internal senses and the possibility of a revelation from the supernatural. This thinking has led to the fallacy that faith resides only in the realm of the emotions and is not grounded in "factual" data.

Let us look at a breakdown of this method. It is highly mechanistic and is fraught with glaring inconsistencies.

1. There are no methods of measuring and evaluating ethical standards.

2. Ethical and moral standards (such as patriotism, bravery, love) are removed from the category of factual propositions.

3. The scientific positivist believes truth is only as secure as the method. So we suffer and endure for a method and not for the actual realities. The experiences are ignored simply because they cannot be classified according to the scientific method.

4. Man becomes a slave of science instead of the master. Man gives up experienced freedom for a theory.

5. Scientific Positivists discount the reliability of meta-physical statements, and at the same time makes use of them. James, the brother of Christ, clearly identified this kind of thinking: "Anyone, then, who knows the good he ought to do and doesn't do it, sins" (James 4:17).

6. The system blindly denies the values of spirit and related values such as joy, faith, love, hope and peace. There are no ideals or moral ideas to live for, thus destroying all meaning and purpose for living.

7. The Positivists relying only on their form of the scientific method contradict their beliefs by their conduct in real life circumstances.

The naturalist undermines the very moral and spiritual vitalities upon which our culture was founded and which alone can dignify man. The method apart from sound morals may develop into a destructive force upon mankind. Scientific reasoning followed to its logical conclusion does not lead to rational thought; it becomes irrational because it does not account for the totality of life.

There are many flaws in this thinking. The Positivist shows a lack of common sense when he denies things, which can be experienced (such as justice, honor, chastity, piety and love). The Scientific Positivists disregard numerous biblical statements:

1. God is Spirit (John 4:24; Luke 24:39)

2. God has given special revelation of Himself to man: Matthew 4:4; 5:17,18; 1 Corinthians 14:37; 2 Peter 1:20,21.

3. God has given revelation of Himself in creation. Psalm 14:1; 19:1; Romans 1:19,20.

4. Conscience recognizes a moral law which man violates. Sin is the result (Romans 3:23; 6:23).

There are many problems the Positivist must answer. Why is there a universal belief in a Supernatural being? What was the first cause in the universe? Scientists elaborate on the "Big Bang" which expanded the universe, but ignore talking about who or what caused the bang. Why does mankind innately worship a being higher than science? When claiming to be seeking truth why is there refusal of valid and concrete reasoning when it contradicts established beliefs? What are you thinking? Is your faith 'reason' or is your 'reasoning" your faith? Have you considered the assumptions that underlie your daily life decisions?

Thinking Questions

1. What is your opinion regarding the relationship of *faith* and *reason*?

2. What is the weakness in using a personal set of standards as the basis for a coherent world and life view?

3. Are you skeptical regarding the possibility of a fully coherent world and life view? If so, why?

4. Do you believe faith resides in the *will* or the *emotions*?

5. Do you presently use a system for arriving at truth?

6. What benefit is there in a supernatural being beyond the realm of our physical existence?

7. Is it possible to have a fully coherent view of our existence apart from God?

8. Is it possible for science to fairly deal with such values as justice, honor, love, hope, joy, faith and peace?

9. Can a scientific philosophy alone guide is in morality? In fact, does morality even exist in a purely scientific philosophy?

10. Read Isaiah chapter one. How does this scripture speak to the relationship of faith and reason? How do you relate faith and reason in your life?

Endnotes

29 Albert E. Avey, "Handbook in the History of Philosophy", pp. 31,32.

30 Young, loc. Cit., p.32.

31 Albert E. Avey, "Handbook in the History of Phiosophy", p. 126.

32 Young, loc. cit., p. 32

33 Avey, loc cit., p. 130, 131.

34 Ibid., p. 192.

35 Ibid.

36 Ibid.

37 Galatians 5:22. The fruit of the Spirit "is love, joy, peace, patience, kindness, goodness, faithfulness, 23gentleness and self-control. Against such things there is no law."

6
The Meaning of Truth

The Interrelation of Truth, Logic, and Semantics

Discovering truth is the object of philosophy. There are many methods used to discover truths. Further methods are used to determine if the conclusions are valid truth. Logic, one of the oldest sciences, is a systematic method of discovering and verifying truth. Aristotle was the first person to set down a system of logic in his treatise called "Organon." This work dealt mainly with deductive reasoning.

Aristotle's logic stood relatively unchanged for 1500 years. The next major step was Francis Bacon's logic of induction, in his work, "Novum Organum." Inductive logic was carried forward in John Stuart Mill's "A System of Logic (1843). His major thrust was "Five Methods for Discovery Causal Relations."

Next we come to "symbolic" or mathematical logic. This is the transition of logic from the actual to the abstract. Symbols are used for propositions, which make it possible to work out relations and equations that are very complex.

Mathematical logic created the necessity for a system to properly interpret the symbols. This led to the field of science now called "semantics." Without the understanding of semantics it would be impossible to grasp the proper meaning when communicating in logic symbols. Logic symbols are used in the field of engineering. Electrical engineers work in the field of electronics where logic is used in connection with various types of electronic memory circuits and software. In the engineering field of Instrumentation in which this author participates, real world control valves, temperature elements, flow and level devices could not function properly without the use of logic language to formulate the proper construction and control in plant processes. System control software is now written using symbols that can create circuitry in computer language that interfaces with the real world of machinery and controls their functions. Engineers would be helpless if they were not familiar with the meaning of this symbolic language.

Criteria of Truth

Seeking after truth has four main divisions: immediate, social, philosophical, and revelational.

1. **Immediate Criteria.** Immediate criteria come through the senses. We learn a large part of our knowledge through the senses. As discussed, some philosophers believe that *all* knowledge comes through the senses. It is true that our senses are the source of a great deal of our knowledge. However, senses are often unreliable, especially our sense of sight. Blinking lights in a sign can appear to be in motion. This author was involved for several years in a "living Christmas tree." An eighty-voice choir sang from a 25-foot tall steal structure shaped like a tree. We programmed the lights using an industrial computer called a PLC. Each year a new feature would be added to the lighting effect. The last effect was garlands of lights draped vertically on the tree, which when programmed for sequential blinking gave the appearance of the tree turning. Information receive through the eye-gate can be an optical illusion. Information through the sense of hearing can also be misleading. The ear hears the

change in pitch of a train whistle, because of the change in position relative to the location of the train. We must conclude that our senses are not the final standard in determining truth. Science would be greatly impeded if the scientist assumed that reality is exactly as it appears to the senses. The knowledge received by the senses must be tested to determine its validity.

2. **Social Criteria.** Social criteria involve the concept of universal agreement. Proponents of these criteria believe, that if an idea has been universally accepted or believed that this is sufficient evidence of its truthfulness. It is impossible to fully demonstrate the universality of an idea. Often this is used to prove the existence of God. Certainly, these criteria may be used with other criteria that might justify this conclusion. However, universal acceptance of an idea by itself does not constitute proof of its validity. A good example might be the once, universally accepted idea of a "flat" earth.

3. **Philosophical Criteria.** This method involves coherence. The definition of coherence is applying the inductive method of discovering truth to the whole of experience. In the scientific methodology, coherence is applied in an idealistic sense:
    a. Consistency – Start with consistent things.
    b. Inclusiveness – All facts must be considered.
    c. Organization – Organize the facts
    d. Hypothesis – Formulate a tentative explanation.
    e. Verification – Test the hypothesis.

"Truth" discovered in this fashion can only be considered probability but it does have merit. This criteria has limitations; coherence can be applied with equal validity to any system of thought. Coherence, or the philosophical method, begins with the supposition that a body of truth exists. The process is somewhat circular. We are striving to validate truths that are already presupposed by the theory. It is difficult to then state that coherency determines what is true.

Where are we in this search? We must come to the conclusion that no matter what the criteria, the whole of reality must be known. Each bit of discovery or probable truth must be tested against the whole. Yet if the whole were known, there would be no search for the truth. It would already be known.

Coherence is only consistent with that which is already believed or previously discovered. Since God is the only one who knows the whole, it would seem to follow that we can only know positive truth through divine revelation, not through self-discovery. Some will argue that the Christian's criteria is no different from the philosophical criteria and has the same limitations. We will leave this question for later discussion.

Revelation as Truth

Although in a naturalistic world, the idea of special revelation is condemned, special revelation must be included as criteria of truth. In an idealistic world, special revelation becomes unnecessary. Men are supposed to have the ability to obtain knowledge of God and His purposes by experience. In a Christian Realistic world, special revelation is an absolute essential.

Christian Realism is built upon special revelation as a fact. The Bible records two types of divine revelation.

1. **Natural Revelation.** This information comes through the world God has created. "since what may be known about God is plain to them, because God has made it plain to them" (Romans 1:19)

2. **Special Revelation.** Special revelation is that communication from God through his human servants so that we may not only understand His workings in our world but also know Him. "All Scripture is God-breathed and is useful for teaching, rebuking, correcting and training in righteousness, so that the man of God may be thoroughly equipped for every good work" (2 Timothy 3:16,17). "And we have the word of the prophets made more certain, and you will do well to pay attention to it, as to a light shining in a dark place, until the day dawns and the morning star rises in your hearts. Above all, you must understand that no prophecy of Scripture came about by the prophet's own interpretation. For prophecy never had its origin in the

will of man, but men spoke from God as they were carried along by the Holy Spirit" (2 Peter 1:19-21).

The Christian world-view is built on a supernatural basis. The Christian Realist stands on the basis of experience. Paul wrote to the Ephesian church, "For it is by grace you have been saved, through faith—and this not from yourselves, it is the gift of God—not by works, so that no one can boast" (Ephesians 2:8,9). Regarding experience, Paul wrote these words to the church at Rome:

> "Everyone who calls on the name of the Lord will be saved." I speak the truth in Christ—I am not lying, my conscience confirms it in the Holy Spirit—...For I am convinced that neither death nor life, neither angels nor demons, neither the present nor the future, nor any powers, neither height nor depth, nor anything else in all creation, will be able to separate us from the love of God that is in Christ Jesus our Lord" (Romans 10:13; 9:1; 8:38,39).

The Christian Realist has the divine guidance of the Holy Spirit.

> "But the Counselor, the Holy Spirit, whom the Father will send in my name, will teach you all things and will remind you of everything I have said to you" (John 14:26). "But you have an anointing from the Holy One, and all of you know the truth. I do not write to you because you do not know the truth, but because you do know it and because no lie comes from the truth" (1 John 3:20,21).

Pragmatism

The term pragmatism was first suggested by Charles S. Pierce (1839-1914), but pragmatism as a theory of truth was not Pierce' definition. William James (1842-1910) took over the term and gave it his own meaning. Pierce quickly disowned the term and coined a new one.

William James was the contributor of the pragmatic theory. James is famous for his work, "Principles of Psychology" which he wrote in 1890. His work is more philosophy than psychology and is pragmatic in its presentation. His theory allows a person to choose and live by the philosophy that fits them best and works. Life is practical and oriented toward the attainment of the greatest satisfaction.[38]

According to James, truth must be determined by its efficiency and for satisfying a specific purpose.[39] In one of James' works he writes, "Truth happens to an idea. It becomes true, it is *made* true by events."[40] This is the basic concept of all pragmatists: It does not work because it is true, but it is true because it works. James defined truth in "over-all expediency in ways of belief and behavior."[41] We reach for truth; it is not absolute. James' view leads to "The end justifies the means."

John Dewey (1859-1952) was a pragmatist, but called his philosophy, "instrumentalism." Dewey believed thinking is solving problems. Without problems, Dewey believed automatic processes took over, or there was what he called, "aesthetic contemplation." Dewey believed we solve most of our problems by outgrowing them. His philosophy saw truth as a continually changing process.[42]

Pragmatic thought rages throughout Dewey's philosophy. Solutions to problems are only true because they work, not because they were always true. A solution that works today may not work tomorrow, so therefore would not be true tomorrow. Dewey was very much a humanist believing there could not be any body of divine knowledge revealed that was unchanging.

Are you thinking? Are you a pragmatist? Do you have abiding truth that you live by and guides your thinking?

Thinking Questions

1. Do you believe you use a criterion of truth in your thinking?

2. Do you consider the Bible to be the revealed Word of God?

3. Is there any justification for pragmatic thinking in the Scripture?

4. Is it possible to know truth?

5. Consider some "beliefs" that you have learned from childhood. Try to list ones that you have accepted without examining or looking for the support for your belief.

6. Have you accepted some of tenets of your faith in a similar fashion?

7. Is it possible to examine our faith using a rational method?

8. Read Romans twelve, verses one and two. Does this scripture speak to having a rational faith?

Endnotes

[38] Albert E. Avey, "Handbook in the History of Philosophy," Barnes & Noble, New york, p. 227.

[39] Warren C. Young, "A Christian Approach to Philosophy," Baker Book House, Grand Rapids. P. 53.

[40] William James, "The Will to Believe" (New York: Longmans, Green and Co., 1897), p. 201.

[41] Albert E. Avey, ibid., p. 227.

[42] Ob sit, p. 253

7
The Nature of Knowing

Throughout our marriage, my wife and I have had a long-standing joke. One of us utters those very important words, "I love you" and the other responds in a kidding fashion, "How do you know?" I started this kidding before our marriage, which was very frustrating to Sharon. She knew I did not doubt her love, but lacking a definitive answer, she would kind of screw up her face and loudly exclaim, "Oh, you!" "Don't do that!" I believe it would be fair to say that since our marriage she has used this tongue-in-cheek statement more than her husband.

I am sure all of us have been questioned at times about something for which we have very strong feelings, and have exclaimed, "I just know!" Knowing is not a simple process. What enters into the process of thinking that brings us to the assurance of knowing? Among some it has been concluded that "knowing" is impossible. There are several "camps" that hold this view.

Agnosticism

Agnosticism was first associated with knowledge of God. Thomas Huxley first used the term in 1869. The agnostic believes there is not sufficient evidence to prove God's existence. Agnosticism has now been extended to all other areas of knowledge.

Skepticism

Skepticism denies that truth is obtainable. Skeptics teach that the rationalist cannot prove his conclusions to be true. They believe their basic postulates are only assumed and cannot be proven. Therefore truth is impossible by deductive reasoning.

Skepticism teaches that conclusions reached by inductive reasoning are based on data discovered by the senses. Since the senses are often unreliable, we cannot know when the data is reliable. Hume was the leading skeptic and carried it into fields of ethics and religion.

There are glaring inconsistencies in the teachings of skepticism. The skeptic claims to know skepticism is true while at the same time maintaining it is impossible to *know*. Skepticism denies even the possibility of knowing. We must believe in the rationality of the mind in order to have a basis for knowing. It may not be possible to demonstrate *knowing* as truth, but there are many ways to affirm the *proof* of knowing.

Positivism

Positivism was formally introduced by August Comte (1798-1857). Comte limited knowledge to what could be derived via the senses. The modern idea is "All knowledge is sense' all else is nonsense."[43] Positivism is a form of skepticism regarding all knowledge not derived from the senses. Positivists would however accept as truth information gained through mathematical concepts.

Phenomenalism

Phenonomenalism is a term often associated with Immanuel Kant. Kant believed knowing is limited to objects of sense experience. He further limited this knowledge to knowing objects only as they appear or seem to appear to our senses. We know the appearance of objects by our sense experience but we do not know its reality. It would appear that for Kant, his view of knowledge is little short of illusion. Kant believed we are still unknowing regarding the metaphysical order. His work "The Critique of Practical Reason," attempted to deal with the metaphysical aspects of knowing.

Monism Approach to Knowing

Monists believe everything is one essential essence, substance or energy. For the monist, knowing equals experience. Reality may be greater than our ability to experience, but identification of the mind with the experience is considered "knowing."

Some monists believe that the qualities of objects exist only in the mind of the perceiver. In other words, "To be is to be perceived." Others, with a more materialistic view, believe that all knowing involves the object. This rules out the spiritual realm. Some monists attempt to relate the object to the process of thinking that goes on in the mind, considering both to be in the realm of reality. It can truthfully be said then, that the monist' encompass both a mystical (mind-reality) and a materialistic view of knowing. Perhaps this can be illustrated by the question of a wife to a husband: "Am I fat?" The mystical monist employing the better part of discretion keeps the quality addressed only in the mind of the perceiver. The materialistic realist answers the question and later wishes he had not.

Dualism Approach to Knowing

Dualism philosophy defines the relationship between mind and matter, which begins with the claim that mental phenomena are, in some respects, nonphysical. The basic tenet of dualism: There are always two distinct aspects to every *knowing* situation. There is the "knowing consciousness" and "the object" of knowing. Perhaps a Sunday dining experience relates this approach. The author, after two days of intense yard work, became extremely drowsy waiting for several persons to prepare dinner at a holiday get-together. Dozing off in a chair, there was a very distinct dream of an industrial pump running, making some very strong clunking sounds. Arousing from the nap, it soon became obvious with open eyes that the icemaker on the refrigerator was being used as glasses of drink were prepared for the meal. At that knowing-consciousness and the object met in the mind of the beholder.

Locke (1632-1704) attempted to clarify this viewpoint. He held that knowledge was comprised of *sensations* that come from the external object and *reflections, which* are internal, in the mind. The sensations were primary qualities such as solidity, extension, and shape, which are inherent in the object. Reflections, the secondary qualities, are such things as color, sound, and taste, which are in the mind of the observer.[44] Awareness of agreement or disagreement between sensations and reflections equals knowing.

The twentieth century philosopher, Edgar S. Brightman, spoke of situations experienced in his form of dualism. Immediate experience is the conscious self. Situations experienced are acquaintances but not knowledge. They represent the immediate data of our consciousness. Situations believed in are objects or situations experienced. Knowing comes through assumptions regarding the experiences after they are classified and organized in light of the experience. Many engineers and scientists are dualists, who seem to not recognize any situation or experience as fact until it is thoroughly classified and placed in a formal proposal. Experiences must be classified in order to accept their validity.

Positive and Negative aspects of Monism and Dualism

Positively, monists contend there is always something in present experience that makes possible knowledge of the past. Generally, monists believe in an all-inclusive or absolute self (very similar to pantheism -God in everything).

Dualism states that a knowing situation is always one in which an idea seeks to know an object. This is the ability of the mind to grasp an object, which is not part of it. Dualism regarding knowing seems to be a reasonable approach. Only God knows the exact way our mind is able to grasp and know objects. As far as it is humanly possible, dualism seems to give an adequate explanation. Keep in mind that the Christian Realist is a dualist; as Christians we know God who is not part of us.

Instrumentalism Approach to Knowing

Instrumentalism is the evolutionary naturalists way of setting forth the problem of knowing in a new way. According to Dewey, knowing is action. As the human organism seeks to adjust itself to it's environment the process of knowing takes place. The naturalist says man is not qualitatively different from the animal. Mind or thinking has developed as man's unique problem-solving instrument.[45]

Instrumentalism would be quite logical if the naturalist's basic assumption were true; the assumption that man is only an animal seeking to adjust to his environment. However, it is easily demonstrated that the differences between man and all other forms of life is highly qualitative, not simply quantitative.

The ability of the mind to Grasp and Know Objects

"A man's goings are of Jehovah; How then can a man acknowledge his way?" (Proverbs 20:24) The average person uses the word, knowledge, frequently. Yet when we turn to the definition of knowing and how the mind knows only a fool says he fully knows or understands what is involved in the process of knowing. Yet, it remains a fact that our mind does know and is able to grasp objects.

My search for answers led me to this question: "When did my knowing begin?" The answer is simple. As a newborn baby I did not know and grasp objects. Contrary to Socrates view, No amount of recollection at that time (unless I believed in re-incarnation) would have brought back to me any inherent knowledge. I brought none into the world. The process of knowing objects is a learned process with only the qualities or functions necessary to know being inherent within the mind.

There is an exception to the above statement. In regard to spiritual discernment, the capability to know God is not inherent in the mind until the Holy Spirit indwells us at the time of salvation. John Wesley spoke, however, of "prevenient grace" meaning that in our natural human state of sin, there is still the ability to respond to the Spirit of God that begins calling us many times long before we acknowledge Him. I want to examine the process of learning beginning with the newborn baby stage.

A baby has no inherent knowledge. A newborn has every sense possessed by an adult but not fully developed. I have heard it said that a newborn baby is unable to see. The inherent ability to see is there; all the seeing part of the eyes, the optic nerve, and connection to the brain is in place. A normal baby has 20/20 vision. He has not yet "learned" what he is seeing. There must be some other connections made before the baby can look at the mother and say, "Mama!" It is only as the senses begin to gather material in their various realms (color, sound, taste, feeling, etc.) and to implant impression after impression on the mind; to sort, organize and file the impressions in the mind for future reference that the mind begins to *know.* It is the sorting, organizing, and ability of the mind to receive and store the impressions that is inherent, not *knowledge* or *knowing.*

Without the use of the senses a child could not know or grasp objects in the mind. The baby's only avenue for learning to know and grasp objects is through the senses. If one were born without any senses functioning, there could be no knowledge conveyed to the mind. Limitation of learning by absence of one or more of the senses will not stop the learning process but certainly increases the level of difficulty. The classic example of one who overcame the lack of two important senses, sight and hearing, is Helen Keller. Though severely limited, she overcame the limitations by using the sense of touch.

A child learns descriptive knowledge. The first words uttered by a child are name words: words such as *Ma-Ma* and *Da-Da.* These words are merely descriptions and are gained through a process of many sounds and sights being transmitted to the mind. When the inherent ability of the mind associates the sounds with the object viewed, *knowledge of description* takes place. At this stage, the child does not have knowledge of purpose or definition.

A child learns definitive knowledge. A baby may be able to name a person or object but does not yet understand purpose, use, or material make-up. A child could be taught that a dog is a cat and believe it whole-heartedly, or that "Ma-Ma" is "Da-Da." These are merely names by which the baby is now able to communicate to another person regarding the person or object. A baby may know that the white thing hanging by the window is a curtain, but does not know it is used for decoration, or to keep out light, or to maintain privacy. The baby does not know whether the cloth is actually "cloth" or fiberglass, and that a loom may have woven it.

In time, a child's many descriptive words begin to be organized. The child acquires information such as the process and its' use. When information such as privacy, decoration, weaving and types of materials is associated with an object like a curtain, definitive knowledge develops. The word "curtain" takes on a far more complex meaning.

This definitive knowledge being stored in the mind for future use comes through all the senses. This information will be the foundation of future decision-making as the child matures. So do not ever think that input into the baby's senses is not important. It will shape their lives. Do you think that the wrong kind of music or argumentative and angry voices do not affect a baby? Think again. Do you think that feeling the abuse of jerking or hitting does not affect a baby or small child? Think again. Do you think that seeing violence or inappropriate behavior does not affect a small one? Think again. When children reach the age that the Holy Spirit can begin to work with their heart they will sort and begin to process a response based on this accumulation of definitive knowledge. Children damaged by the process of a negative definitive knowledge base may have a hard time responding to spiritual input and arriving at right decisions.

There are principles necessary to the learning process inherent within our minds. Remember that knowledge is not inherent in the mind, but we are born with the capable process to learn. We have certain set principles:

- **Attention:** "One of the more obvious characteristics of perception is its selective nature. At any given moment our sense organs are bombarded by a multitude of stimuli. Only a few of these stimuli are given a clear channel. We perceive clearly only a very few events at one time. Other events are perceived less clearly, and the rest form a sort of hazy background . . .This is another way of saying that, of the various events around us, we attend to only a very few. So attention is a basic factor in perception."[46] And therefore, a basic factor in knowledge. We hear a great deal today concerning "Attention Deficit Deficiency." Attention is of great concern today in the development of a child.

- **Shifting of attention.** "The fact that we do at some time hear the conversation behind us and do notice the coldness in our feet illustrates another aspect of our field of attention. Attention is constantly shifting . . .What is it that determines what we will attend to?"[47] Although attention does shift there is orderliness in the shift. It is not completely chaotic. If it were only chaos we should be unable to carry on any extended activity. There are certain principles that determine the direction of our attention.[48]

    o Intensity and size. The louder a sound the more likely a person will attend to it. The brighter the light the more likely it will capture our attention. By the same token we will more likely notice a full-page advertisement than we will a half-column one. In the same way, a baby seeks the brighter of two objects and more quickly sees a person than an article of their clothing.

    o Contrast. As human beings, we tend to adapt or become used to the stimulation around us. The annoying ticking of a clock that may be noticeable upon entering a room fades into the background after longer exposure. When the ticking stops abruptly we become immediately aware of the silence.[49] We quickly become aware of any rapid change of stimulation in our environment.

    o Repetition. Anything continually repeated is more likely to be perceived. Repetition of a word to a baby will more quickly cause the baby to perceive that word and correlate it with an object.

o Movement. Anything moving in our field of vision attracts our attention. Unbelievable as it may seem, if someone walks into our field of vision when watching a favorite show or sport on TV our attention is drawn to that person.

o Motives. The first four principles of attention are external stimuli. Inherent processes make all people react in the same manner. Motives are internal stimuli. One example is hunger. A baby experiences hunger pangs. Although the baby does not understand them, the infant soon learns that the bottle of milk or a mother's breast will satisfy.

o Set or expectancy. This is a learned process. The mind will in some way adjust to this process. A sound or noise we are expecting may awaken us quickly, whereas a normal sound we are not expecting may not arouse us. An example: a very sleepy doctor hears the phone ring but is not awakened by the sound of his child crying.

Our minds perceive objects external to our mind. "One of the most obvious facts of our perceptual experience is that it is filled with objects. The stimulation that we are constantly receiving comes into our mind as shapes and patterns."[50] Our sense organs "tend to organize or modify our perceptions into simple patterns or objects. The measured ticking of a clock is usually not heard in that fashion. We tend involuntarily to accent the even "tick, tick" and perceive it as "tick-tock.""[51] Such organizing tendencies are somehow built into the way the sense organs and nervous system function. There are names given to these organizing tendencies: grouping, figure-ground perception, contour, closure, and apparent movement (neon-bulb signs). The Greek builders were masters at utilizing this principle as it pertains to illusion. The grand Parthenon structure in Athens appears to have evenly spaced columns surrounding the edifice. The distances at the corner columns have been modified so the columns appear to be evenly spaced, but in fact, they are not.

John R. Ingram

The fact of illusion is another proof of the inherent processes of our mind in dealing with stimuli and learning correctly. Our mind is capable of determining true stimuli even when our senses do not agree with the data. One example is a stick thrust into the water. It appears to be bent to the sight stimuli, but upon feeling it (touch stimuli) we find it is not bent. We can prove our mind's decision by taking the stick out of the water and seeing that now both the stimuli of sight and the stimuli of touch agree; the stick is straight. How about you; "How do you know?"

Thinking Questions

1. Do you have firmly held beliefs you cannot explain?

2. Can you remember when they became part of your belief system and why?

3. With which 'camp' of knowing do you identify?

4. Perhaps we all have had a period in our life when we were somewhat agnostic in our thinking. Discuss that period in you life and why.

5. How does agnostic thinking differ from skepticism?

6. Can you identify areas of skepticism in your thinking?

7. Have you known individuals who believe they have inherent knowledge? No need of external input? How would you describe their relationship with others?

8. Magicians base their work on illusion. Do you have beliefs in the framework of your thinking that may be illusion?

Endnotes

43 Young, loc. cit., p. 63
44 Young, loc. cit., p. 76.
45 Ibid., p. 70.
46 Clifford T. Morgan, "Introduction to Psychology", p. 163.
47 Ibid., p. 169.
48 Ibid.
49 Ibid.
50 Ibid.
51 Ibid.

8

The Nature of the Universe

Metaphysics

In looking at the nature or origin of the universe, it is necessary to look at the science of essential principles. That science is metaphysics. Metaphysics is that branch of philosophy that is concerned with the real. The philosopher asks, "What is real?" There was certainly this sense in the question put to Christ by Pilate, "What is truth?" Related questions in this realm of thought are,
- "What is the nature of being?"
- "How did the universe originate?"
- "What is human personality or consciousness?"
- "What is the ultimate purpose of existence?"

We may not have phrased the questions quite in this fashion in our lives, but I dare say, no one is a foreigner to the nature of these questions. Dr. John Stott, of England, while speaking to pastors at Wheaton College, related that all persons seek three things in life: To know God, to have worth, and to be loved. In regard to worth, I have often walked out under a glorious night sky in the lane of our country

81

home, and asked God, "What is the purpose of *my* existence?" "Why was I born?" This personal soul-searching cannot ignore the larger questions of metaphysics, the very nature of our being and the origin of the universe.

There are traditionally four sub-branches of metaphysics, and I would also add a fifth one:

- **Ontology -** The study of being
- **Cosmology –** The study of the Universe
- **Psychology –** The study of the soul
- **Theology –** The study of God
- **Axiology –** The study of all types of values.

There are differences among metaphysicians concerning the nature of reality and differences regarding the extent of reality. Most agree upon the nature of the physical world, but others question whether nature is all there is to reality.

Early Greek Metaphysical Theories

The earlier Greek thinkers could be considered to be monists for they sought one principle to explain the nature of things. Among these were:

- **Thales** (624-550 B.C.) This early Greek thinker believed water to be the basis of all things. He arrived at this by what he had observed, and "his answer was the result of his own thinking."[52] Aristotle believed Thales belief was based on his observation of the power and importance of water in life and its quantity. Thales was the first hylozoist. This is one who believes in the theory that all matter is alive.

- **Anaximander** (611-547 B.C.) Anaximander carried on Thales' thought but made a great stride forward. He reasoned that if we look for a substance underlying all phenomena of experience it could not be some particular form of matter like water, but would be unrestricted, unlimited in its' nature. "In saying this he anticipated the position that is held at the present when men speak of 'energy' as something which assumes various forms under different conditions, such as heat, light, magnetism, and molecular agitation."[53]

- **Anaximenes** (588-524) Anaximenes took a step backwards in his search for the basis of reality. The thinking of Anaximander (too far ahead for his day) was rejected in favor of an "empirically observable substance, air as the ultimate form of reality."[54]   It should be apparent that all three of these thinkers excluded the spiritual realm from the circle of their reality.

The following groups of Greek thinkers are pluralists regarding reality. Again, they do not give place for a creator-god.

- **Empedocles** (492-432 B.C.) Empedocles held that earth, air, fire and water made up all things. These basic elements he believed were controlled by the forces love and hate. "The universe undergoes a cyclic process of evolution and devolution as one or the other force dominates [sounds like some marriages]. Empedocles held that biological evolution came about through the random combination of organs and then the elimination of those unfit for survival."[55] So you thought Darwin originated "survival of the fittest!"

- **Anaxagoras** (500-428 B.C.) Anaxagoras took Empedocles theory further, believing the number of pluralism of reality was not four, but an infinite number (one for each quality), which he called *seeds*. These were controlled by *minds* (another term for God) that set the universe in motion originally.   His thought was not unlike some who were later called Deists. Deists believe in a supreme being, but that he did just that; set everything in motion, and is now a disinterested god.

- **Democritus**(460-370b.c.) Democritus set forth an atomistic materialism. Things were made up of many atoms of the same quality, different in size and shape. The motion, or the motivating force was inherent in the atoms.

These early Greek thinkers definitely made strides forward in understanding reality even though there were many fallacies in their theories. With a few exceptions, the majority were naturalists in thinking, eliminating the idea of a supernatural force.

In a Christian approach to thinking and understanding truth we cannot eliminate the influence of God's word. Although the Greeks were great thinkers they are still to be held accountable for not seeing a divine controlling being in all reality. They are without excuse when they tried to eliminate God from their equations. Democritus is a prime example. He taught that motion, the beginning of reality, was inherent in the atomic particles of nature. The apostle Paul summarizes this humanistic thinking in his letter to the Roman Church:

> Since what may be known about God is plain to them, because God has made it plain to them. For since the creation of the world God's invisible qualities—his eternal power and divine nature—have been clearly seen, being understood from what has been made, so that men are without excuse. For although they knew God, they neither glorified him as God nor gave thanks to him, but their thinking became futile and their foolish hearts were darkened. Although they claimed to be wise, they became fools. (Romans 1:19-22)

Definition of Substance

We want to look at three men, Locke, Berkeley and Hume (1711-1776), and their definition of substance (and we are not talking about drugs).

First looking at John Locke's definition we find it may be the "un-cola" of philosophy. He believed that matter or substance is unknowable, but that we can know certain qualities that adhere to it. He divided these qualities into two groups:

- **Primary qualities** –Locke believed these qualities exist in the object itself.
    - o Solidity
    - o Extension

- o Figure
- o Gravity
- o Motion
- o Rest

- **Secondary qualities**
  - o Colors
  - o Sounds
  - o Tastes
  - o Feeling
  - o All sensible qualities besides the primary (apparently a catch-all, or as it would be called in industrial projects, a contingency).

Locke believed the actual object (matter or substance) could not be known immediately; we could only know the impression that it made upon our mind.

George Berkeley "dismissed Locke's distinction between primary and secondary qualities as being untenable, hence he rejected Locke's doctrine of an underlying substance apart from the perceived qualities. Berkeley believed things are exactly as we experience them.[56]

David Hume carried empirical sense to the extreme. He agreed with Berkeley and drew the same conclusion regarding the spirit. Hume reduced all experience to "impressions" of sense and "ideas" which are the lingering image of them. Hume believed we do not perceive our own bodies. We only have sense impressions of them. Perhaps Hume was on to something. I certainly know some individuals who for various reasons, drugs or otherwise, are out of touch with their bodies! He believed there is no mind, but only a collection of perceptions falsely believed to be endowed with "an underlying personal identity."[57] He denied any causal relationship of any matter or substance. In short, he denied a Sovereign God. "Thinking themselves wise, they became fools."

Gottfried Leibniz (1646-1716) coined another name for the basic substance of all matter – Monads. He believed these "monads" were living and dynamic. He believed they were conscious centers of force. Some were classed as sleeping monads (probably philosophy 101 students) that would comprise inorganic matter. Leibniz was a hylozoist; one who believed inherent in all matter is life. Reality was made up of these conscious centers of force, and there is no causal relationship between them. All apparent causal connections and relationships exist because the Monad of Monads set them in order from eternity. How greatly the philosophers struggle to not clearly identify the Supreme Being as God. I have another name; He is Lord of Lords and King of Kings!

The Nature of Substance in Modern Science

In the fourth chapter, we discussed the contrast of philosophy and science. Essentially, science discovers, philosophy relates. I cannot emphasize enough the importance of keeping these tasks separated between these two disciplines. Relationship begins to involve purpose, and it is not the job or scope of science to define purpose. The naturalists, or humanist who denies the existence of a supreme being would like to make science the supreme god, and believe within its hallowed courts lay all the answers to life. Not so. In spite of many false directions in philosophy, it is still the commission of man to find relationships and ultimately, wisdom, outside the scientific hall of learning.

In the scientific realm, science is continually looking into the nature of the physical universe. Present day science is advancing so fast the average person finds more confusion in their conclusions than advancement in knowledge. In chemical and medicinal areas, it seems that as soon as a study is done that promotes a new chemical for medical purposes, another one comes out to refute the evidence.

There are some "probable truths" that we usually accept. Science has demonstrated that matter is composed of 109 elements. These elements, assembled in various ways, comprise our physical world. The atomic theory, held since the time of the ancient Greek philosophers, has been determined to be a "probable truth." No one has seen or observed an atom, but only the effects of it. For example traces of electrons have been seen or rather the path of electrons has been seen in such apparatus as the Wilson Cloud Chamber.

This indirect verification of atoms is similar to search for impurities in the production of high-grade silicon for use in computer chips.

While leading an instrumentation project at a major producer of high-grade silicon, in 1991, the changes and removal of chemical piping and valves created impurities showing up in the final product. Expecting plant support for my project, I found myself working very much alone, as all plant personnel were thrown into support of the chemists to find the impurities. They could not be seen; they were in infinitesimal amounts that could not be found by our finest instruments. They had to be tracked down by the "impressions" and other conditions they caused within the product.

All the elements are comprised of atoms which are like tiny solar systems; the nucleus of the atom likened unto the Sun, and positively charged; the electrons revolving around the nucleus, negatively charged, and likened unto the planets revolving around the Sun. The nucleus is comprised of a certain number of protons and neutrons that are held together by strong cohesive forces.

The electrons present in an atom vary with different elements, ranging from hydrogen, which has only one, to Meitnernium, which has 109. There is considered to be a relatively great distance between the nucleus and the revolving atoms. It is said that if the nucleus of an oxygen atom were magnified to a diameter of 1500 feet and placed at the geographic center of the United States, the outer electron in this atom will travel in an orbit, one side of which is New York City, and the other side of which is San Francisco.

The atom is a complex building block of matter. The complexity varies with different elements. Some of the parts of the atom are the electron, the positron, the proton, the neutron, the mesons, hyperons, deuterons, neutrinos, and antiparticles. Recent studies in Canada and Japan have revealed that neutrinos may be the basic building blocks of all life. They have determined they have mass and change over time.

The Role of Philosophy in Relation to Substance

Science is discovering more everyday about the building blocks that make up our world. It still remains for philosophy to relate these new discoveries with all of reality. The continuing debate over stem-cell research and issues such as abortion seem to rise and fall on the viewpoints of scientists and philosophers (and I include Christian teachers under the latter, as we are hopefully still "lovers of wisdom - seeking it with our whole heart). The scientist who is a humanist has no qualms about the aborting of an embryo, as it is not yet considered to be "life." And after all, the scientist has determined that science is the supreme truth and becomes god. The philosopher, depending on beliefs, will have a wide range of responses to these ongoing debates. Yet it is important to not allow these issues to be decided in the halls of science. Science must remain the discoverer, not the interpreter of substance, and hence, life.

The Christian realist does not condemn true science. He believes it will never contradict the revelation of God if it is a true discovery. However, the Christian must continue to hold as the standard of truth and authority, God's authoritative, verbally inspired Word. Although to the secular mind this may seem arrogant, when science disagrees with a biblical perspective or truth, the Christian relies on the Scripture and holds the scientific view to be erroneous. The above discussion of the atom should caution us that much in science is only "probable truth" and in some cases such as the hotly debated issue of evolution, only a theory which has never been proven to be true. In fact, science has stepped over the line from discoverer to interpreter of life in regard to evolution and determined that this is their "blind leap of faith." Science has become a 21st century religion of the masses, many blindly following, believing they hold the keys to all truth.

Evolution is a theory no less, yet most educational systems and the courts of our land treat it as fact. A number of school systems are challenging evolution being taught as the only possibility to explain mankind's origins. Several are advocating teaching "Intelligent Design" as an alternative. This was recently challenged in the courts; the plaintiff's claiming it is just a ruse to teach religion in the schools. The plaintiff's were supported by the federal judge's decision that used very derogatory words directed at the intelligent design proponents.

> In one of the biggest courtroom clashes between faith and evolution since the 1925 Scopes Monkey Trial, a federal judge barred a Pennsylvania public school district Tuesday from teaching "intelligent design" in biology class, saying the concept is creationism in disguise.

U.S. District Judge John E. Jones delivered a stinging attack on the Dover Area School Board, saying its first-in-the-nation decision in October 2004 to insert intelligent design into the science curriculum violated the constitutional separation of church and state.

The ruling was a major setback to the intelligent design movement, which is also waging battles in Georgia and Kansas. Intelligent design holds that living organisms are so complex that they must have been created by some kind of higher force.

Jones decried the "breathtaking inanity" of the Dover policy and accused several board members of lying to conceal their true motive, which he said was to promote religion.

A six-week trial over the issue yielded "overwhelming evidence" establishing that intelligent design "is a religious view, a mere re-labeling of creationism, and not a scientific theory," said Jones, a Republican and a churchgoer appointed to the federal bench three years ago.[58]

In regard to "substance" natural scientists avoid reality. When origins of the universe or matter are discussed, scientists "don't go there." They begin with matter, attempt to explain matter, but not explain its origin. Discussion of matter is buried under so many layers of complex explanations it is difficult to recognize it is based on the premise there is no god. At least some of the Greek thinkers went so far as to see some "Unmoved Mover" or "Force" that was eternal behind the creation of all matter.

A humorous story received recently from a former Christian Navy buddy serves to illustrate the avoidance of substance-origins. A scientist was talking to God and told him. "We don't need you anymore." "We have discovered how to create life." God said, "Oh, is that right?" Can you demonstrate this for me?" Willing to oblige, the scientist said "Of course!" "I just need to gather a little dirt." He bent down to scoop up some dirt, when God stopped him. God said, "Get your own dirt!"

Someone said that the atheist has difficulty in finding God for the same reason a thief cannot find a policeman.

Many theories long held by scientists are being proven false. Many who are finally seeing the logical idiocy of no supreme being have come to believe in a God standing behind all of creation. All science is not false. It can bring to light incredible discoveries, and has advanced the knowledge of man in many ways. In regard to science, as Christian thinkers we must follow the admonition of Paul: "Prove all things; hold fast that which is good. Avoid oppositions of science falsely so called. Which some professing have erred concerning their faith."[59]

Our Universe: Finite or Infinite?

In answer to this question, the Christian Realist must answer that the universe is finite. God is creator of the universe according to the Scripture. God is infinite. Since the universe was created it had a beginning. It is therefore, not infinite in time.

The question of the infinite conveys two aspects: space and time. The universe, first of all is not timeless. Creation means a beginning. The Word of God also emphatically declares, "Heaven and earth shall pass away, but my words shall not pass away" (Matthew 24:35).

Although the universe is not infinite in time, could it be infinite in space? Could not an infinite God throw His created universe and infinite distance in space? Perhaps time is considered to limit the distance of the universe. Because of it's finite existence in time one could argue that an infinite space would require an infinite time to exist. But did not Christ who is God, pay an eternal payment for sin in a finite time, which man could only pay for eternally? Could not this same God create an infinite space in a finite time?

There are two "proofs" from the scientific realm that the universe is finite. In the modern theories regarding astronomy, the theory is the universe is finite, and came into existence from one mass about three to four billion years ago. This was arrived at through a study of light waves from distant nebulas that are very much like our own galaxy. The nebula (like our own Sun) are approximately 100,000 light-years in diameter, and they are spaced approximately ten times that distance from each other.

> When the light from these distant nebulas is passed through a spectroscope, the lines of familiar elements are observed. The lines from the distant ones are shifted slightly toward the red end of the spectrum. According to the Doppler effect, this would mean that these nebulas are moving away from us. An example of the Doppler effect is observed in sound. When you pass a sound such as a bell, while riding on a train, the pitch of the bell drops, and the faster the train is traveling, the greater is the change in pitch. The curious fact that develops is that, the farther the nebula, the faster it is receding.[60]

By the study of this effect, scientists determine by reversing the process that the universe began about 15 billion years ago according to present scientific "knowledge."

This is a very accurate scientific process, but it depends on a basic assumption that the rate of acceleration of the universe outward from its origin has remained constant since it began. It is possible that God could have *thrown* the universe into space at a greater rate of speed, or even that He created it at a greater distance from the *center* of the universe. Scientists also assume the universe all began at the same point (its center) from which all the stars, planets, etc., are diverging.

This is evidence that the universe is finite both in space and time, but it does not constitute proof for the age of the universe. The basic assumptions are out of the realm of scientific investigation and therefore cannot be proven. God is not limited; He did not have to begin the universe at one common origin, nor did the acceleration speed have to be constant from the beginning of time.

In agreement with the astro-physicists estimate of age, another process claims to demonstrate that the universe is finite. Carbon 14, a radioactive element, is used in the study of plant photosynthesis. Carbon 14 disintegrates at a fixed rate so that its presence in organic material theoretically enables scientists to determine the age of these materials. It is thought that carbon 14 is formed naturally in the atmosphere when neutrons from cosmic rays bombard nitrogen atoms in the atmosphere and cause the formation of new unstable nuclei. This in turn disintegrates, leaving Carbon 14.

Plant and animal tissue actively absorbs Carbon 14 from the atmosphere as long as it is active. When this tissue dies, it has been found by experiment that the absorption of Carbon 14 ceases. By this method, physicists have arrived at an age for the earth, which approximates that of the astronomer. Again, the theory is based on the assumption that the rates, the half-life, the rate of absorption, have always remained constant. Since this is not demonstrable it cannot be proven. In fact, until the recent Canadian and Japanese experiments with neutrinos, they were considered to be constant, with no mass and unchanging. We now know neutrinos change over time and have mass. In the Scriptures, there is evidence that the heavens (atmosphere) were changed which would have changed the rate of absorption of Carbon 14 and possibly even the rate of disintegration.

From the Genesis account we know the earth originally was watered by a mist and not rains until the time of the universal flood. When the rains began, it was something entirely new. This certainly constituted some change in the atmosphere, to bring about a new type of watering system. Peter speaks of this in his second letter:

> But they deliberately forget that long ago by God's word the heavens existed and the earth was formed out of water and by water. [6]By these waters also the world of that time was deluged and destroyed. [7]By the same word the present heavens and earth are reserved for fire, being kept for the day of judgment and destruction of ungodly men (2 Peter 3:5-7).

Again, Carbon 14 is an evidence of a finite universe, but not a confirmation of the *age* of the universe.

The Problem of the One and Many

The problem can be summarized by these questions: "Is there anything in common among all the phenomena of reality?" "Is there not some connection between the many diverse facts of the universe?" "What one principle gives meaning to existence?"

The first approach to this problem is quantitative. Is the world one or many in number? Monists believe that reality is one being – Any pantheistic system whether of the idealists or materialists type would belong to this category of thinkers. For example, materialism asserts that the only thing in common among all real things is matter. The materialist believes there are only material connections between the many aspects of the universe.

Democritus (460-370 b.c.), the Greek atomist, is an example of a quantitative pluralist. He believed all things were composed of neutral entities in which the motivating force was inherent in the atoms, a subtle form of pantheism.

Is there a synthesis of monism and pluralism? The Christian realist believes there are both the one and the many. There are many things in the universe quantitatively speaking, but they exist and are controlled because of the one, who is God. The revealed Word of God is the only "philosophy" that has a consistent, coherent answer to this synthesis.

The bible asserts that all things have in common the fact that they were created by God, that they are connected by a purposeful relation to the mind of God and by the power of God through which all things consist.

> For by him all things were created: things in heaven
> and on earth, visible and invisible, whether thrones or
> powers or rulers or authorities; all things were created
> by him and for him. [17]He is before all things, and in
> him all things hold together.[61]

The meaning of life is realized when one knows, believes, loves and obeys God, the Creator, the Savior.

Is the world one or many in quality or kind? Some naturalists and materialists believe that reality is only matter. Idealists are also monists, for they believe that reality is only spirit. Idealists assert that the only thing in common among all real things is idea or mind; all the facts of the universe are connected by the one vast mind that is reality.

Dualists believe there are two kinds of substance. Plato believed in two worlds existing together: a world of essences, and a world of matter (the receptacle of the essence). Seeing the receptacle (matter) was not actually seeing the essence. The Christian believes in two substances: Spirit (God) and matter that were created by God out of nothing. Christians are therefore contingent dualists (one of the two depends upon the other for existence), not eternal dualists. Some dualists believe that matter and spirit are co-eternal, matter being equated with evil, and spirit with good. There are certainly traces of this belief in the Gnostic teachings that sprang up in Judaism as well as early Christianity.

Humanity's Limitations

In an early writing for a course in philosophy, before man had achieved orbit or landed on the moon, I composed an article, entitled "The Possibilities of Space Travel." There were still many skeptics even in the decade of the sixties who doubted man would ever escape the bounds of earth's gravity and soar into the heavens. My father was one of those persons.

Let me say at the outset that he was a brilliant man, multi-talented in many trades, but did not have the benefit of higher education. He left school in the 10th grade to help support a family of two brothers and three sisters, his mother, and an ailing father. My father was a realist. He was a committed Christian. However, with his lack of scientific knowledge, he believed that a rocket engine would never be able to fly in the vacuum of space because it "would have nothing to push against." This may seem an absurd notion to many who have had the privilege of greater knowledge and education. Yet it is not a belief any more absurd than theories developed by the materialist or agnostic. Those who have not had the privilege of "higher education" in spiritual truths, and have not come face to face with the creator of the world propose far greater absurdities.

In Genesis 11:6, we read, ".nothing they plan to do will be impossible for them." This was man's earliest attempt to reach the heavens. The Tower of Babel was being built by mankind to "reach the heavens," a rebellious reaction to humanly achieve protection and "god-like" abilities without divine assistance. They said to one another,

> Then they said, "Come, let us build ourselves a city, with a tower that reaches to the heavens, so that we may make a name for ourselves and not be scattered over the face of the whole earth (Genesis 11:4).

Shortly after the writing of my article on space travel, the radio and television regularly broadcast these words: "The launching this morning at Cape Kennedy was a total success. The satellite is right on course, responding perfectly to all controls. All systems are go!" A few years ago, language that was only heard in the realm of science fiction is now commonplace. Recently, two robots, controlled from earth, roamed the hills and valleys of Mars, and the pictures were available for viewing worldwide on home computers. There are now hundreds if not thousands of man-made satellites whirling around our globe, and it is a common task to daily view the weather patterns from space. A private company has just now achieved space orbit and projects having "space hotels" and private moon travel within a generation.

Space travel was met with the same skepticism as all significant steps in scientific endeavors. Many said, "Man will never go to the Moon," just as the said, "Man fly – Humbug!" or "A steamboat?" "Just Fulton's Folly!" "Sail around the World?" "Never!" "The World is flat!" Yet man goes on to prove whatever he purposes to do he is able to accomplish. Yet how long will God permit these advancements? Similar arguments are being applied today in other areas of research: cloning of human beings, and artificial intelligence, to name just two.

The man who said we would not reach the moon, or other planets, stated this for one of two reasons: First, he either knew so little about science that he was ignorant of the possibility, or he believed God would not permit it. I do not have or claim to have the knowledge or omniscience to say how far God will permit man to travel in space, or the omniscience to say God will not permit it. However, God's Word is very clear that man achieves only what God sanctions.

The incident of the Tower of Babel in the Old Testament, although not high-tech, gives us the principles that we can use to understand what God will permit mankind to accomplish. The Genesis account parallels space travel endeavors. Man attempted to reach heaven by means of a physical building so that God could no longer overthrow the human race and scatter them.

Now the whole world had one language and a common speech. As men moved eastward, they found a plain in Shinar and settled there. They said to each other, "Come, let's make bricks and bake them thoroughly." They used brick instead of stone, and tar for mortar. Then they said, "Come, let us build ourselves a city, with a tower that reaches to the heavens, so that we may make a name for ourselves and not be scattered over the face of the whole earth." But the LORD came down to see the city and the tower that the men were building. The LORD said, "If as one people speaking the same language they have begun to do this, then nothing they plan to do will be impossible for them (Genesis 11:1-6).

Note, that man was united for one purpose. He was building a city and a tower whose top would reach heaven, for the purpose of making a name, and maintaining unity. We read in verse four, "Come, let us build ourselves a city, with a tower that reaches to the heavens, so that we may make a name for ourselves and not be scattered over the face of the whole earth."

Today, the entire world is not united. There are many divisions and existing strife between countries. It is interesting however, that countries unite to achieve space travel, such as the building of the international space station. There is some unity today, in the face of terrorism, united in ways to cooperate to wipe out the terrorists cells. The union generally centers around threats to sovereignty of nations and the destiny of the world. Truths in the Genesis account may be applied in all such endeavors.

The Scripture also speaks of a coming day, when once again, the world will attempt to unite in a common cause, rallying under the leadership of the Antichrist, to establish his sovereignty and fight against Christ's return on the Day of the Lord. There have been attempts to unite nations. The failed endeavor, The League of Nations was formed to once and for all end all wars. The United Nations, a similar organization, attempts to bring unity and understanding to nations. In the final days of this age rallying under the ensign of the Anti-Christ, there will once again be a union of nations, characterized by the same rebellious spirit of those gathered at the Tower of Babel project.

At the time of Babel, there was one race of people on the earth, survivors from the great Flood. They spoke one language. Language has always been considered a great barrier. Today, there are two uniting factors coming in to existence: common language and economic union. This union is developing across national and political boundaries. The early race had great unity because they shared a common language.   In verse six of our passage, God makes it clear that the very purpose of their project was to make a name and maintain their unity. This united humanity would certainly not have reached the heavens with their bricks and mortar, but they could have continued a rebellious unity of purpose if God had not intervened. God is not against unity, in fact desires it for all who will follow in His teachings. What He is opposed to is a unity without faith; the kind of unity he opposed by barring man from the Garden of Eden and the Tree of Life after they had sinned and were no longer a pure and holy creation.

When the space race began, after the first Russian success with "Sputnik," the goal was set to achieve superiority in space. It was believed that superior power would enable the winner to control the destiny of their country, and perhaps the world.   Motives were the same as the gathering at Babel.

The peoples at Babel were one race, descending from the survivors of the great flood. They spoke one language. God states they had begun their work, and there was nothing that could limit them form achieving any purpose which they determined. The last phrase of verse six is significant. Three words are important: *nothing, restrained,* and *imagined.* "Nothing" is translated from two words in the Hebrew, which approach the Greek idea of a double negative. Rather than cancel the negativism, it is used for emphasis. We could literally translate the words, *not-nothing.* Rather than bad grammar, in Hebrew it is all-inclusive; without God's restraint, man can accomplish all he plans.

The second word, "restrained" means "inaccessible by *height* or *fortification".* The united people without divined intervention would not be restrained; they could reach any height or breach any fortification. The final word, "imagined," means just that. Whatever they devised or schemed would be accomplished as a united people if God did not intervene. After man sinned in the Garden of Eden, they were banned from the place so they would not eat of the tree of life and live forever. Man was not to have eternal life apart from purity of life. In the same fashion, God has placed limitations on mankind as long as we are in our sinful state.

What do you think? How far can mankind travel into space? How far can mankind go in genetic manipulation, in cloning, or any other imagination devised? How great and to what extent will there be economic union? The only limitation is the extent of almighty God's permission.

Thinking Questions

1. Have you spent time thinking about the purpose of your existence?

2. Have you often felt there is a vacuum inside of you that you struggle to fill?

3. Have you tried to fill it with relationships?

4. Do you agree with the words of Paul to the Romans that God's qualities can easily be seen?

5. What role do you believe science should play in understanding life? Can truth be found exclusively in the halls of science?

6. Should the public classroom be limited to the teaching of evolution in regard to origins?

7. Do you believe there is one principle that gives meaning to existence?

8. What do all things have in common according to Scripture?

9. Is it possible to find purpose in life apart from God?

10. What parallels with the story of Babel can you see in today's thinking?

Endnotes

32   Albert E. Avey, "Handbook in the History of Philosophy, New York: Barnes and Noble, p. 11.

33   Ibid.

34   Ibid.

35   Ibid., p. 15

36   Young, loc. cit., p. 76

37   Handbook, p. 154.

38   By MARTHA RAFFAELE HARRISBURG, Pa. (AP) -

39   1 Thessalonians 5:21; 1 Timothy 6:20,21

40   Richard Wistar, "Man and His Physical Universe, New York, John Wiley & Sons Inc., 19__, p. 144-146.

41   Colossians 1:16,17

9
Where Did it All Come from?

Have you ever sat and just thought about where you came from? I don't mean how you were born. Where did "stuff" come from? How did any "matter" come into existence? Perhaps I could ask this question in a reverse manner: Did you ever sit and try to imagine or think of "nothingness?" Try to imagine non-existence?" It can be very depressing, and quite frankly, I believe beyond the capabilities of our human mind.

Influenced by the Hebrew Scriptures, the belief that all things of whatever form were created by an act of the eternal and infinite God remained unquestioned for millenniums. Eventually, numerous thinkers challenged the act of creation by God out of nothing.

Early Greek Views

Thales (624-546 B.C.) conceived of everything being derived from water. Some process produced life during the drying up of the earth and the appearance of the landmasses. There is nothing new under the Sun, as some still believe in some form of "spontaneous generation" of life out of waters. As late as the 1970's when teaching elementary school, this author was given a slide show for science class to show to the 6th grade. The "science unit" was teaching the spontaneous generation of life from the waters of the Nile River. It was promptly returned.

Anaximander (610-546 B.C.) suggested that life came from terrestrial slime. Ambiguous Heraclitus (date) taught that everything flows and nothing abides. Anaxagoras conceived of Nous (mind) as bringing about order and development in a chaotic universe.

Empedocles (490-430 B.C.) focused on the existence of four basic elements —earth, air, fire, and water, which are acted upon by the influence of love and hate. The law of chances determined the end result.

Aristotle (384-322 B.C.) spent nearly 20 years in Plato's academy, under his tutelage and then as a teacher. He became a traveler and educated a famous pupil –Alexander the Great. He taught the doctrine of development. An intelligent force called Pure Form controlled the process. Lower forms, under the control of Pure Form developed into higher forms. Aristotle did not suggest a theory of evolution to explain the development process.

Note one thing common to all these early theories: none of them speak of where substance or material came from in the first place. They did not go there. Scripture teaches God created out of nothing. Some of the early philosophers and certainly some today would say matter is eternal; it had no beginning. It is impossible to honestly approach this area of origins, beginning with nothing, and not accept the existence of a Supreme Being, an infinite creator. We are really faced with two choices: either nothing created out of nothing, or God created out of nothing.

Evolution

History repeats itself. Much as in the days of the famous Scopes trial, one of the hottest debated issues today is evolution. Since this theory impacts directly on our thinking regarding origins, it is necessary to review this theory.

Theories of evolution have not progressed far from the early Greek assumptions. Evolution is a theory of process, not a theory of origins. It must be emphasized it is still a theory; it cannot even be graced with the level of probability. Evolution is the Holy Grail of science; the blind leap of faith. Within this "religion" it is acceptable to disregard tried and true methods of scientific discovery.

Emergent Evolution comes closest to looking at the origin of matter. This theory assumes that the eternal and basic stuff of existence is Space-Time, from which all else has emerged. From Space-Time (the real) emerges matter; then after a long process, life emerges. In the continuing process, the various forms, as we know them, emerge. Finally, from human life emerges *Mind*. Then –here comes the leap of faith- from *Mind* emerges *Deity* or the *Unknown*. Some supporters of this theory believe it is a spontaneous process, while others have brought some controlling factor back into the method. Some have conjectured a vitalistic principle or divine activity. Lloyd Morgan (1852-1936) held this theory.

Many professing Christians have held to some form of theistic evolution. God used the process of evolution to create. Note that emergent evolutionists theorized the "divine" proceeded forth from the mind of the evolved human. It was not a vital principle that set it all in motion.

Theistic evolutionists were quick to adopt evolution and bring it into the sanctity of faith, accepting the idea that Scripture was not meant to be a scientific book. They accepted evolution as the process or methodology which God used to bring to pass the various forms of life. The days in Genesis one are considered to be long time spans, not twenty-four hour periods. They did not want to appear to be ignorant of the scientific world, and succumbed to vigorous attacks on the traditional view of millenniums that God created out of nothing.

Organic Evolution deals strictly with the development of the process. It is defined as "a continuous natural process of racial change in a definite direction, whereby distinctively new individualities arise, take root, and flourish alongside or in place of original stock."[62]

Some would define evolution as the development that may have taken place within the great kinds or families in the plant and animal kingdoms. All the flies, felines, canines, etc., are thought of as having a common origin. That all forms of life, both plant and animal, originated in one or at the most, in a very few sources of life, is the most widely accepted belief among scientists. There are both philosophers and scientists who hold to *no* evolution, *partial* evolution, or the *complete* evolution of living forms.[63]

In regard to the theory of evolution, there are a number of common terms. *Acquired characteristics* are changes that have been brought about by environmental conditions. It is theorized that environment increases or decreases usage of certain organs of an animal by means of habits. The changes are then transmitted by inheritance. It must be noted that this theory was completely disproved by August Weisman (1834-1914), an embryologist, in experiments with germ plasma.

Natural selection was advocated by Charles Darwin, who published his ideas of natural selection in 1858) and Alfred Russell Wallace (1823-1913). This theory promotes the idea that nature produces an over-abundance of individuals; more than nature has room for or can nourish properly. A tremendous over-production results in a vast majority being killed. Because of the crowded condition, a continual struggle for existence is in process. In this struggle, *survival of the fittest* takes place. Those with the superior characteristics will survive, while others die off. The survivors transmit the favorable characteristics to their offspring that results in the selectivity of nature.

This theory requires many "missing links" for which ample evidence has never been produced. Although lacking scientific evidence this theory is taught worldwide in schools and universities as fact. *Mutation* is a change in the genes of an organism. Other changes are also seen in the chromosomes. This theory is advanced because it eliminates the "missing" missing links. Many eminent scientists still do not believe this accounts for evolution.

From the realm of mathematics and secular science comes a challenge to Darwinian evolution. Recent controversy over ID, intelligent design, focuses on the tenacity of the scientific world to continue the separation of faith and reason, which rests squarely upon the "faith" that evolution is simply the evidence of a mechanistic universe. A recent article by John Wilson, "Science in Wonderland," shares in tongue and cheek fashion, the following words:

> Faithful readers of the *New York Times* will recall historian Garry Wills's op-ed, "The Day the Enlightnment Went Out," published immediately after George W. Bush's reelection in November 2004. for a

time, it appeared that Wills's dire pronouncement was merely the sober truth. Attempts were being made to smuggle Intelligent Design into America's classrooms. But the forces of Enlightenment rallied. One weekly science magazine featured a cover story with this stark warning: "The End of Reason?" *Wired* magazine joined the fray with a cover story devoted to "The Plot to Kill Evolution." *Rolling Stone* chimed in with a banner headline, "Science vs. Faith: Evolution on Trial." The rest is history. According to a recent story in the *Times,* Reason is resting comfortably and is expected to make a full recovery."[64]

The tongue in cheek continues as he discusses the incredible scientific grasping for the apparent absurdity of a universe such as ours developing in a chance fashion. Thinking scientists a few years ago came forward to admit the extreme improbability of all the conditions required for life being just so for life to happen. Some went so far as to hint at some form of creation. In answer to this new "attack on reason" the "string theory" was born.

Some began to argue that our universe is but one of an unimaginable number of universes, say 10 to the 500th power, in which case the features of any one universe (ours for instance) are unremarkable.[65]

This parallels methods sometimes used in industrial control systems. If the existing system does not work properly, instead of finding the problem, another layer of control is added, that somehow is believed to have the capability to correct the previous error. If it is not credible that Darwinian evolution had time to take place, then let's theorize innumerable "strings" of universes" to provide the possibility of chance happenings not found in our universe that will somehow make the faulty theory plausible. Not all secular scientists have given approval to the "string theory" but neither do they express any incredulity. Yet, Mechanistic scientists become alarmed and intellectually blast the slightest suggestion of intelligent design.

Charles White, in an article, "God By The Numbers," identifies the absurdity of ruling out intelligent design simply by looking at known facts of mathematics and clearly lays to rest Darwinian evolution. Even if one accepts the date of the "Big Bang" theory, as taking place about 15 billion years ago, it can clearly be demonstrated by modern methods that Darwin's theory of mutations did not have enough time to happen. White's correct numbers identify that,

> For Darwin's theory to have a chance [just a chance!] of being right, the universe would have to be a trillion quadrillion, quadrillion, quadrillion, quadrillion, quadrillion, quadrillion, quadrillion, quadrillion, quadrillion, quadrillion, quadrillion times older than it is. Because the universe is so young [even if that age is 15 billion years] Darwin's argument fails, and William Paley's contention that design presupposes a designer becomes more persuasive.[66]

It is difficult to read these factual and reasoned approaches to the controversy without it coming to mind that perhaps much of the scientific world can be described as "straining at a gnat and swallowing a camel."

Evaluating Evolution

Evolution has many unanswered problems. First we must consider the origin of life. Evolutionists believe that at some time, "brute matter is assumed to be able to evolve by itself into living matter."[67] This process cannot be demonstrated to have taken place. In space exploration, such as in the recent Mars Landers, rocks and materials are being examined to try to find the transition of matter to living forms. The theory of spontaneous life is fraught with many obstacles.

- **All life comes from life.** The basic building block of all life forms is the cell. The cell multiplies by division into two equal parts. All cells originate from cells. All parts of the cell come from parts of other cells.

- **No chemical process has been discovered to explain the origin of life protoplasm.** In spite of this, it is still being taught as factual in many early elementary textbooks. There is an egg present in all life that arrives by a form of reproduction. It is impossible for organic life to antecede itself.

- **Sudden appearances of fossils in the Cambrian period[68] seem to uphold an immediate creation.** In this period there is an abundance of fossils of great variety, while the preceding period yields no evidence of any true life forms. Although many theories have been presented, evolutionists have never brought forth any evidence for the existence of life before the Cambrian period.

This is the true picture: In the pre-Cambrian era, little evidence exists for fossils of any kind. In the Cambrian period, there are fossils in abundance of all the phyla (def). The abrupt appearance of so diversified fossiliferous evidence in the Cambrian period cannot be accounted for by the evolutionary hypothesis, but would fit perfectly the assumption that the original ancestors of all life forms arrived by some sudden creative act.

- **One Primal form.** Evolutionists have not been able to reduce all living forms to a system that would show that life came from one primal form. Evolution cannot scientifically furnish a completely integrated and unified system. This is their "leap of faith." In a deceptive manner, the theory is still put forth identifying this development from a primal life form as fact.

Comparative anatomy is another field that has been manipulated by the evolutionist. *Homology* is the investigation of basic structural similarities in the field of comparative anatomy. Organs may be externally different, yet possess similar internal structure. The use of that organ, however, may vary between different life forms. Examples of hololeous organisms are, the wing of a pigeon, the flipper of a whale, or the arm of a man. Homology is used as a satisfactory means of classifying plants and animals.

107

Analogy is the opposite of homology. Organs are analogous when unlike in structure but used for similar purposes. These similarities of structure are assumed to show common ancestry. Structural similarities are said to result from the process of development.

Inheritance and *variation* involves a difficult problem for the evolutionist.

- **Inheritance transmits similar characteristics.** Similarities in homology are supposed to be explained by inheritance.
- **Variation is a diversifying process.** Deviation of usage and adaptation of homologous organs are supposed to be explained by variation.
- **Neither inheritance nor variation is consistent in these processes.** Inheritance both simplifies and diversifies, while variation converges and diverges.

Paleontology is the study of the forms of life existing in prehistoric or geologic times, as represented by the fossils of plants, animals, and other organisms. Fossil evidence found in various strata of rock are said to support evolution. Older rocks, or strata are said to contain simpler forms of life. The newer strata up the geological time scale are said to contain fossils more closely related to present, existing life.

As I understand this system, I remember a cartoon strip from the fifties, called "Myrtle." Often Myrtle's boyfriend walked her home after dark, to "protect" her. Then he is afraid to go back home because of the dark. So she walks him back home. The geological scale is a "merry-go-round." The fossils that are found in the rocks establish the geological time scale. Then the rocks are arranged in the order on the scale to represent fossil evidence found from the simplest to the more complex. This specific rock order does not exist in the natural world as we examine the strata of rock laid down in areas throughout the world.

An article by R.H. Rastall, in the Encyclopedia Britannica, acknowledges this circular argument:

> It cannot be denied that from a strictly philosophical standpoint geologists are here arguing in a circle. The succession of organisms has been determined by a study of their remains embedded in the rocks, and the relative

ages of the rocks are determined by the remains of organisms they contain.[69]

Somehow, by reflecting that this argument is in the realm of the philosophical, it can be excused as not having scientific weight. Love of Wisdom; has it all fled away?

The evolutionist builds his "organic" tree of life. It branches off into two great stems: the New World and the Old World monkeys. From the latter in recent geological history (according to the evolutionist) man proceeded. Modern evolutionists believe in some ancestor that is common to both man and the apes.

Throughout the years, there have been many specimens used to "prove" this theory of the evolution of man. Many "proofs" have been brought forward to show different forms of man at various stages of development. The "proofs" have been fragmentary bones from all over the world. There has been no consistent agreement regarding these specimens. Some have considered them to be entirely human, while others have believed them to be entirely apes.

It is incredulous, in this arena of science and philosophy, that such a vast number of scientists accept evolution lock, stock and barrel, even though no conclusive evidence has ever been brought forward to prove it. The majority of those accepting the theory have not had uniform agreement on the deciphering of the "evidence." A good example would be the cranial capacity of the so-called "Piltdown Man." After assembly of the cranium area, estimates as to the actual capacity have varied as much as 430 c.c.

Darwin published his *Origin of Species* in 1859, and yet no one today has any clear knowledge of the origin of a single species. As previously noted, the theories laid down by Darwin would not have had time to take place in our "young universe." In the study of man, there is no evidence that man did not possess his intellect from the very beginning.[70] One link with the past is language, and the basic forms of our language seem to be as old as man.

Many set out to reject the idea of creation in favor of evolution, which leads to many theories and contradictions. Rather than accept a divine creation that fits all the known facts and erases inconsistencies, the evolutionary theory is assumed to be absolutely true. Then, the evolutionist sets about to solve all the theories and contradictions. In many cases, inconsistencies are simply ignored, choosing rather to take the blind leap of faith.

The creationist believes that man and ape are different in kind, and that common ancestry is impossible. There are essential differences in behavior. These consist of:

1. Only humans make artificially. Other animals make things, but purely by instinct. There is no noticeable difference in an animal product from generation to generation. Humans show originality.

2. Only humans think when it is not necessary to do so. The philosopher, John Dewey would disagree, believing humans only think when confronted with a problem. Unfortunately, in some cases he would be correct. Many individuals do not use their god-given creativity to arrive at new ideas. They simply exist. Perhaps a better way to state this distinction would be that humans have the *capability* to think even when they are not confronted with a problem. This difference results in humans being able to communicate ideas.

3. Related to the second distinction is freedom. Humans exercise free choice. Humans are the only rational beings. For example, we choose various ways to live together.

Many fossils show similarities between humans and animals physically, but that does not cancel the fact that humans and animals differ in kind. What it does show is the evidence of a common creator-God.

In regard to development and ages, many scientists believe in uniformity and slow geological changes. The evidence does not seem to uphold this theory. Again, science has chosen to make a theory supreme, then set about to prove it. In the process, they completely ignore or twist information to fit their assumption.

Uniformity theories do not in any way fit or harmonize with Scripture, or the development of the earth as seen in the study of the earth. Only divine creation of all things, and sudden changes such as the Genesis flood are consistent with the Word of God *and* the evidence at our disposal in the realm of geology.

Unfortunately, many Christians have given way to the pressure of the gods of science. Dr. Strong, of *Strong's Concordance* fame, almost apologized for Christian scholars who used the Scripture as the final authority of creation. He wrote,

> We grant the probability that the great majority of what we call species were produced in such ways. If science should render it certain that all the present species of living creatures were derived by natural descent from a few original germs, and that these germs were themselves an evolution of inorganic forces and materials, we should only be required to revise our interpretation of the word *bara* in Genesis 1:21 and 27 and to give it there the meaning of mediate creation, or creation by law. Such a meaning might almost seem to be favored by Genesis 1:11, "Let the earth put forth grass."[71]

Although this quote is from a book from the early 20th century, it expresses the position of many Christians today. This belief places our faith upon the faltering foundation of science and not upon the Word of God. Strong continued in this text to state that the theory of long periods rather than literal days is not inconsistent with the biblical account.

What are you thinking? Many Christians seem to be embarrassed to disagree with secular science on the basis of the teachings of God's Word. The argument goes something like this: "It is foreign to the purpose of revelation to teach science." Somehow, this statement is supposed to harmonize the differences between the Bible and the alleged truths of the natural sciences. Is it not interesting that the word, "science," comes from the Latin word, *scio,* which means knowledge? The Word of God is about knowledge: knowledge of God, knowledge of man, and knowledge of the universe. The Word of God can be trusted in every discipline to speak the truth, and the Christian should challenge the scientists to seek explanations that support the clear and concise teachings of direct creation by an almighty God.

The Scriptures -the Word of God- give a more detailed account of the origin of life than the entire evolutionist writings put together. In Paul's letter to the Thessalonian church, he exhorts them to "Test everything. Hold on to the good. Avoid every kind of evil" (1 Thessalonians 5:21). To his spiritual son Timothy, he writes, "O Timothy, keep that which is committed to thy trust, avoiding profane *and* vain babblings, and oppositions of *science* falsely so called: Which some professing have erred concerning the faith" (1 Timothy 6:20,21). Let us not err in our faith, but know that we can trust the Word of God, the revelation that has stood the test of time and changes lives.

Thinking Questions

1. What does it mean in terms of our human level of thinking that God created out of nothing?

2. What element is common to the early Greek views of origins?

3. What fear among Christians led to the acceptance of theistic evolution?

4. Apart from belief in a divine creation can there be any answers to origins?

5. Why does modern science and education refuse to address the unanswered problems of evolution? For example, there is no chemical process to explain the origin of life-protoplasm.

6. Do we have knowledge of the origin of any species?

7. In this postmodern world what is gained by a "blind leap of faith" and not honestly addressing origins?

8. Explain the basic difference between the uniform view of the development of life and an act of immediate creation? Which view is supported by known facts of geology?

9. If the Bible is the true revelation of God what is wrong with this statement: "It is foreign to the purpose of revelation to teach science."

Endnotes

63 Text, p. 89.
64 *Christianity Today*, "Science in Wonderland," April, 2006, p. 74.
65 Ibid.
66 *Christianity Today*, "God By The Numbers, p. 46ff.
67 Young, ibid., p. 93.
68 This is a geologist's method of naming evolving earth ages. It is a circular argument, for it is determined primarily by the fossil life found in the rocks, then in turn the rocks are arranged in a sequence to demonstrate the evolving order of life. The sequential strata of rock in accord with the geological theory, does not appear in this sequence anywhere on earth.
69 *Geology*, The Encyclopedia Brittanica, 1956, Vol. 10: p. 168.
70 Young, loc. cit., 101
71 Strong, Systematic Theology, p. 391-395.

10
Are You in Your Right Mind?

What is my mind

Psychology is the science dealing with the mind. The term comes from the words psyche, which means soul, and the word logos, which refers to study. Psychology in the simplest definition is the study of the soul. Don't let the definition fool you; most psychologists do not believe the soul exists. Soul is simply believed to be the interaction of the organic make up of our brains chemical and electrical reactions. Try teaching that to an avid blues singer!

Psychology later became related to the word consciousness, and more recently, the word behavior. Behavior is that aspect of a person that can be observed. Why is psychology the study of "behavior"? Why not "mind" or "thought" or "feeling?" The answer is simple. You can only study what you can observe.

We know that there are events going on within a person: events that can be called thoughts, feelings, or perhaps mental activities. We can and do make fairly trustworthy inferences regarding these events, but we always make them from the way a person behaves. It is what a person says, does and writes that scientists can record. A person's inner processes of the mind, thoughts and feelings, can only be brought to light through a person's behavior.

Therefore, psychology cannot tell us the exact nature of the mind; only report on its activity by behavior. Some of the teachings of psychology might lead you to believe otherwise, but the problem of the nature of the mind, soul, or spirit is still with us. Modern psychologists cannot explain the psyche or explain it away.[72]

Historical views of the Mind

The Greeks are considered to be the first ones to make efforts to formulate a doctrine of the soul or consciousness. This view, of course, ignores the writings of the Bible, by the Hebrews, long before the epoch of the Greeks.

Democritus taught that mind is made up of the finer, smoother material atoms of which reality is composed. Heraclitus believed reality was an eternal process. He believed our senses testify to substantial objects but reality is in eternal flux.

Anaxagoras taught reality is made up of an indefinite number of elements that do not explain the world of experience. The *nous* (mind) is the control behind the ordering of the world.

Plato believed man to be a tri-part personality; reason is in the head, courage is in the chest, and appetite is in the abdomen. He believed the soul of man was eternal, and since the physical nature limited the soul, the physical should be dispensed with. The physical nature was not considered a part of the personality.

Aristotle believed the soul to be twofold: "There is the active soul, and the passive part, or soul substance, in which the active soul resides. The active soul comes from the world of forms and is eternal but all functions and activities of the body perish with it."[3]

Modern Psychology

John Locke believed Man's mind at birth is a complete blank. All knowledge comes from experience. Experience equals sensations, (man's awareness of external objects) and reflections (the minds operation on sensations and other reflections).

George Berkeley taught "To be is to be perceived." There is no material in which certain qualities reside, but all qualities reside in the mind of the perceiver. Mind or consciousness is the only existing realities.

David Hume rejected any causal relations, believing the perceiver only accomplishes relationship. "Reality, he concludes, is nothing but a chain of ideas, supported by no abiding substance and connected by no necessity.

Imananuel Kant agreed with Locke that experience comes through the sense gate, but the mind itself gives order and meaning to the experience. Kant said knowledge must be limited to the phenomenal order — the world experienced by the senses, thus denying an actual knowledge of the supernatural world. This would be true if it were not for the illumination of the Holy Spirit.

Locke's psychology initiated two lines of thinking: 1) School of associationism; thought is nothing but the putting together of simple ideas. 2) Psychological Scepticism. This Arose from the distinction made between primary and secondary qualities. Locke (1690) wrote, Essay Concerning Human Understanding.

Hume was the first *associationist* in Psychology. Associational psychology rejects the conscious unity of an abiding self in favor of a self as a bundle of sensations or ideas.[73]

Behaviorism

The term *behaviorism* can be attributed to John Watson of Johns Hopkins University. His definition eliminates such terms as soul, mind and consciousness in psychology because of their subjective nature. His concept of behavior is the response of organs to stimuli, both internally and externally. He does not distinguish between human and animal responses, qualitatively. "Human personality is to be understood entirely in terms of stimulus — response activities or conditioned reflexes resulting in habitual action."[74]

Memory is only the ability of mind to retain habits after non-activity. Watson defines personality as "the sum of activities that can be discovered by actual observation of behavior over a long enough period of time to give reliable information. In other words personality is but the end product of our habit systems."[75] Therefore, we are no different in our responses than animals are in theirs.

The behaviorist seems to ignore some existing facts such as a conscious inner life. John Dewey believed the mind only was thinking when confronted with a problem. But thinking often originates in the mind, without external stimuli, and sends an impulse from the brain, which sets in motion a physical response. Behaviorists have only dealt with the reactions and not the source. They have closed their eyes to introspective psychology, that which looks inward upon the state of consciousness, and declared it does not exist.

Self-Psychology

According to personalists, *mind* is consciousness. Therefore, since mind is not a substance, it cannot be separated and analyzed in different ways. The mind experiences itself in the present, together with past-consciousness, and groups past with present as belonging together. In other words it gives to the stream of consciousness, past and present the unity that is personality. The self, or person is the conscious experience taken as a whole.

Self-experience is time-transcending. The conscious self is able to connect the "I" of the past, present and future as one and the same "I". Personal identity is maintained through time.

Self-psychology is presupposed by memory. The remembered experience and the memory are both seen as belonging to the same self, the same organic whole of conscious life that belongs together.[76] Yet, one must ask, "How can the conscious life be organic when it is not substance, but only self-existence?"

Self-psychology is presupposed by thinking. Logical reasoning of the mind is considered to be the same as mind or conscious self. The ideas conceived, and the conclusions are both related to the same "I" of consciousness.

Self-psychology is presupposed by *values*. Only "persons" "value." The idea of values implies a "valuer".

This view of psychology includes no idea of an abiding self. If consciousness is self, then unconsciousness is non-self. Therefore, in the unconscious state, the *self* would cease to exist. There is not an abiding self, that exists when not consciously uniting memories, or conscious clusters of past, present and future.

The Abiding Self

The personalistic self-psychologist believes the human self ceases to be when in a state of unconsciousness. The self, then, is dependent upon consciousness for it's existence. Therefore, self is consciousness. But if this were true, then self is temporal, and at times nonexistent, making the possibility of immortality seemingly impossible. Whew! Better read that several times! How some people think!

The *realistic* self-psychologist believes the *abiding self* is the actual self that continues in spite of unconsciousness. It is that part of man which gives unity to the flowing, fluxuating stream of conscious life. When the personalistic self-psychologist takes the abiding self out of psychology, he no longer has "psyche-ology", but "psyht-ology", only that which he can see.

Getting the mind and body together

There have been dualistic thinkers who have wrestled with the relationship of spirit and body. They have tried to parallel them, striving to maintain a complete separation. Descartes was one of these, but in face of the overwhelming evidence to the contrary, was defeated and did not maintain a strict parallelism.

Spinoza was another who called spirit "thought" and matter, "extension." He concluded these were two of the infinite attributes of God, which flowed out of God; the only two men can know. There is no relation between thought and extension, but every point in one corresponds to parallel points in the other, just as two objects might be exactly the same height, but have no connection or relationship.

Inter-actionism cannot be done away with. Psychologists know that certain mental conditions can and do effect a person's physical condition. Railroad tracks are parallel, never touching each other, but they are connected all along the way by wooden ties. A train could not run for long on these rails if they were not connected, for their distance from each other would vary and cause the trail to derail. That mind and body definitely have interaction can be seen by the simplest thought of the mind that brings about a physical reaction. This is something humans cannot explain so they try to do away with it. As a Christian realist, I cannot explain it; I merely accept it.

What is Christian Psychology?

The Christian realist does not eliminate the original definition of psychology, *the study of the soul*, but relates it with *mind* and *behavior*. This gives an organizing unity to psychology, which is not possible apart from the *abiding self*, or *soul*.

The Bible speaks many places concerning the mind, which when studied give a sound basis for Christian psychology. Although the Christian allows for the abiding self, there must be a purpose for this mind to follow, to give direction through the complicated maze of life. There is a direction in scripture that finds its purpose in Jesus Christ.

Christian psychology is Christ-like psychology.

Explaining the essence of our mind or *abiding self* is beyond human capability but does not prove it is not existent. The behaviorist writes it off as just a physical interaction. The mind is real and is often spoken of in the scriptures. Denying the existence of mind is denial of God's Word.

Though the mind cannot be fully explained or examined, it can be guided and controlled. This control comes from a source external to the mind. This is not slavery of the mind or forced obedience. It is just the opposite: it frees the mind for the mind is its own slave. Is there any greater slavery in thinking that indetermination or lack of direction? This external source gives us determination and direction -direction towards a purpose. It can be summed up in six words: "For me to live is Christ."

Our Mind is controlled by Obedience to Christ.

"For the weapons of our warfare are not carnal, but mighty through God to the pulling down of strongholds; casting down imaginations (reasoning) and every high thing that exalteth itself against the knowledge of God, and bringing into captivity every thought to the obedience of Christ."[77]

Our minds find their direction and purpose in Jesus Christ. In Ephesians chapter two, verse thirty-one we learn that before spiritual birth, our minds are carnal, fulfilling desires of the flesh. Our minds are "puffed up" and full of pride (Col. 2:18). Obedience to Christ is the direct opposite of the sin of pride.

Obedience to Christ is impossible apart from spiritual birth. Our natural mind is blinded by wicked works (Col. 1:21). When we are spiritually born anew Christ reconciles us. The spiritually born person is converted. A complete change in direction takes place in the physical life and in the mind. The spiritual birth is a complete about face, from a carnal, puffed up, pride-filled mind to "serving the Lord with all humility of *mind*" *(Acts 20:19)*. Paul wrote to the Colossian church, "Put on therefore, humbleness of *mind*" (Colossians 3:12).

Christians can be great hypocrites. We tend to take out the bad habits and forget the "I", that abiding self. It is *self* that stands in the way of serving God and becoming all that He wants us to be. The Bible teaches *self-denial*, not denial of *things*. In evangelical circles the "law of the Pharisees" often takes precedence. They continually sought to be approved before God by addressing their actions and not the self within. Christians too often want to focus on a so-called Christian life of self-righteous good works. Paul said it was not his fleshly works that serve God but the mind: "So then with the *mind* I myself serve the Law of God" (Romans 7:25). Christ said the first and greatest commandment was not —do good works (I don't smoke, I don't drink, I don't chew, and I don't run with those who do)- but that we should love the Lord our God with all our heart and with all our soul, and with all our *mind* (Matthew 22:37). The term recorded in the Greek is διανοια, that means "the understanding mind."

IF we, therefore, love God with our minds, we will serve the Lord with humility of mind. Again we are directed to Christ. In Paul's letter to the Philippians, Paul writes, "Let this *mind* be in you which was also in Christ Jesus, who though equal with God, humbled himself, and became obedient, even unto death" (Philippians 2:3). With that *abiding self* in us, which is the presence of Christ, we will esteem others better than ourselves. This is humility of *mind*.

A person who illustrated this humility of mind throughout his life was Samuel Morris Jr. Sammy was a young black man who was saved in the jungles of Africa in the late nineteenth century. Directed by the Lord, he came to America to study. He came to prepare to serve the Lord in ministry. What he may not have known at the time was his entire life was one of service.

He enrolled at Taylor University. Unfortunately, in those days, even among Christians, there was concern over a black man rooming with other white students. At the beginning of the semester when room assignments were being made, the dean summoned Sammy to his office. Before the Dean could really say much about the concern over arrangements, Sammy spoke up and said, "Sir, any room will be all right. Is there a room, maybe just a closet, that no one else wants?" "Give me that room." How many of us are willing in our mind to take the room no one else wants? How many of us have that humility of mind?

When Jesus comes in, the sinner's life and mind is changed. The new person sits at the feet of Jesus. Legion, out of whom Christ cast the devils, was such a man. "And they came to Jesus, and found the man, out of whom the devils were departed, sitting at the feet of Jesus and in his right *mind*" (Luke 8:35). His mind was transformed. Jesus told him to go witness and he willingly obeyed.

Our Mind is Controlled by Purpose – to Please God

When St. Paul pleaded his apostleship before the Galatians he wrote, "Do I now persuade men, or God? Or do I seek to please men? For if I yet pleased men, I should not be the servant of Christ" (Galatians 1:10). Many live their lives trying to please others. Because of the utter hopelessness of the task the failure causes great frustration.

The Christian's goal should be to please God which is not impossible; it is possible through Jesus Christ. We must always remember that it is only through faith that we can please God or the frustration will be as great as in the struggle to please men. "But without faith it is impossible to please him: for he that cometh to God must believe that he is, and that he is a rewarder of them that diligently seek him" (Hebrews 11:6). Through the pleasing of God the spiritual desire of the mind can be obtained. The result is satisfaction of attainment rather than the hopelessness of frustration. The glory should be for God, not for man. Man fails; God cannot fail, for He is God.

Our Mind is Controlled by Organization – Simplicity in Christ

"But I fear, lest by any means as the serpent beguiled Eve though his subtlety, so our minds should be corrupted from the simplicity that is in Christ" (2 Corinthians 11:3,4). Many people today engage a psychiatrist to clarify and sort out the complicated maze of their mind that has become so entangled in worldly wisdom and desires. Life is truly complex. Negotiating all the areas of society, business, and just daily existence is akin to walking through a minefield. In today's fast paced life styles confusion often reigns and leads to nervous breakdowns. Failing to find purpose or direction for the complexities of life are the major cause of this condition.

For the Christian realist, Christ gives simple, straightforward clarity of all life's existence. "For me to live is Christ." The path through a jungle maze may be clearly marked, and bring the explorer safely to their destination. If the path is disregarded, there will be encounters with tangles of vines, trees, swamp, and dangerous animals. Christ requires, simple, steadfast trust, following Him. He is the path. Jesus said, "I am the way, the truth and the life; no one comes unto the father but by me" (John 14:6). We must follow and stay focused.

Our Minds are Controlled by Focus – Stayed on Christ

The universal prophet Isaiah, a seer who saw Christ's day in the 8th century B.C., wrote, "Thou will keep him in perfect peace whose mind is stayed on thee; because he trusts in thee." (Isaiah 26:3). Jesus Christ is the goal for the spiritual person. He is the guiding purpose of life's existence. If the mind is not stayed on Christ the Christian wanders into sin and confusion because the mind wanders. We can maintain our obedience of mind to Christ by keeping our mind full of the teachings of the Scriptures. David understood this principle: "How shall a young man cleanse his way? By taking heed thereto according to thy word. Thy word have I hid in my heart that I might not sin against thee" (Psalm 119:11,12). The focal point of the Christian life is Christ. "Let us lay aside every weight, and the sin which does so easily beset us, and let us run with patience the race that is set before us, *looking unto Jesus the author and finisher of our faith*" (Hebrews 12:1,2). Let us run by faith, in His strength, and continue to run.

We Control our Minds by Renewal

In Romans 12:1,2, we are exhorted to "be transformed by the renewing of your mind" so that we can comprehend the will of God. This renewal is continual. Paul feared lest the Corinthian church would be drawn away from the truth of the Gospel. He marveled that the Galatian church in a few short months had departed from the truth. He wrote this with great anxiety of heart while on his journey Back to Jerusalem. "I marvel that you are so soon removed from Him that called you into the grace of Christ unto another gospel" (Galatians 1:6). There was no other gospel, only a perversion.

Renewal is not a new gospel, but renewal of the same Gospel of Jesus Christ. The renewal is a renewing of the mind concerning the truths of Christ. It is study of the Gospel that becomes more precious every day. Jeremiah wrote of the Lord's mercies, "They are new every morning" (Lamentations 3:23).

Renewal and continual control of our mind takes place by dwelling upon the true Gospel and avoiding the false Christ's. Paul had strong language for the imposters: "But though we, or an angel from heaven preach any other gospel unto you than that which we have preached unto you, let him be accursed" (Galatians 1:8).

Renewal is by knowledge of the Lord. IN 2 Chronicles 15:1-8, the account is recorded of Oded, the Prophet going out to meet Asa, King of Judah, after a victorious battle. He prophesied to him concerning the Lord's intervention in the affairs of Judah, and the promise that his work would be rewarded. This word to Asa gave him the courage to clean up Judah. He focused on renewing the altar of the Lord.

Oded's prophesy has it's counterpart in 1 Corinthians 15:58, the last verse of the great resurrection chapter. After Paul proclaims to the Corinthians the promises of the resurrection, he writes, "Therefore, my beloved brethren, be ye steadfast, unmovable, always abounding in the work of the Lord, forasmuch as you know that your labor is not in vain in the Lord." The knowledge brought to Asa caused him to abound in the work of the Lord, and the Chronicler writes, "The heart of Asa was perfect all his days" (2 Chronicles 15:17).

We too, can be perfect of heart and mind by knowledge of the hope of the resurrection and eternal reward for our labors, being perfected by the knowledge of the Son of God. We will no longer be like little children, tossed to and fro, and carried about with every wind of doctrine by the sleight of men and cunning craftiness; no longer having our minds darkened by the blindness of our heart, but growing up, obeying Christ, looking steadfastly toward Christ, continually renewing our minds so that we may prove what is that good and acceptable and perfect will of God.

Thinking Questions

1. What part does psychology play in understanding who we are?

10. Psychology is in reality a branch of science. How does the study of human behavior relate to psychology as a science?

11. Are psychologists, especially behavioral psychologists, guilty of the same extension of their trade as other scientists —assuming the role of interpreting and not simply discoverers of truth?

12. Read over the views of modern psychologists regarding the mind. Can you identify with a particular view?

13. Do you believe in an "abiding self?"

14. Give your definition of Christian Psychology.

15. What differences would take place in your life if your mind was focused on God?

16. Is it possible to fill the void or lack of self-worth in our lives by a relationship with a friend, lover or spouse?

17. Define the purpose of your life.

18. Do you believe you must know God to have purpose?

Endnote

72 Young, loc. cit., p. 105
73 Ibid., 110
74 Ibid., p. 112.
75 John Watson, *Behaviourism*, New York: W.W. Norton & Co., 1924, p. 191.
76 Ibid, p. 114
77 2 Corinthians 10:5

11
What Has Value

We are living in a very different world in regard to an understanding of *value* or *values*. In this postmodern world, language has changed. The definition of *value* has changed. However, it is not simply a problem of linguistics; it is an entire cultural shift, as well as a breakdown of the underlying belief system. For some, there is no such thing as value; life is meaningless. The modern definition will be explored, but first, let us look at many traditional definitions of value.

H. Hoffding (1843-1931) defined value as the property possessed by an object either by conferring immediate satisfaction or serving as a means of procuring it. John Laird (1805-1874) described it as the conditions necessary for the maintenance of an entity. R.B. Perry (1904-) saw value as the peculiar relation between interest and its object. R.A. Tsanoff (date) felt it is easier to show where value is found in personal response to experience, no matter what general form that experience may take.

Edgar Brightman (1884-1953) described value as whatever "is liked, prized, esteemed, desired, approved, or enjoyed by anyone at any time."

Warren C. Young described value, as "something liked by someone at some time."[78]

Types of Values

There are two types of values; *instrumental* and *intrinsic.* Instrumental values lead us to other values and are considered the *means.* Intrinsic value is valued for its own sake. It is the *end.* Pure instrumental or intrinsic values are rare. Most values that are instrumental (means) would also contain qualities making them intrinsic (end).

The Wisdom of Value

What reasoning stands behind your standard of values? Here are several theories attempting to explain the psychology of value.

Hedonism is the doctrine that pleasure or happiness is the highest good. The word is derived from a Greek word meaning *pleasure.* Many teachers, both past and present, have held that pleasure alone motivates a person's actions. What is pleasure has value; what is not pleasure is of no value. Hedonists still discriminate between good and bad pleasures. If this theory were true, it still would not prove that it should be true.

Voluntarism teaches that whatever satisfies desire or fulfills purpose is of value. For example, a pragmatist might say, "a true value would be one which brings about a successful course of action."[79] Another way of saying this would be, "The end justifies the means." This would make the value both instrumental and intrinsic.

Formalism teaches there is nothing good except the good will (Kant). True value (not the hardware store) is found in the rational will itself. Value is found, not in the consequences of an act, but only in the right principle behind the act.

The coherent theory relates all the previous theories, maintaining there is some merit in all of them. Coherence strives to relate value to the whole of the personality.

Value Classification

Values are also grouped into "lower" and "higher" classifications. The "lower" ones are considered narrower and more practical than the "higher" ones. The "higher" values are considered broader, and more inclusive of experience as a whole, more independent, and more coherent.

1. Values considered Lower
    a. Values such as health and hygiene.
    b. Recreational values, play, recreation, amusement.
    c. Work values. Tasks that make life possible.

2. Values considered Higher
    a. Social values. Values produced by associative and sharing behavior.
    b. Character values. The conscious choice of what is believed to be right and best.
    c. Aesthetic values. The beautiful, the sublime, the tragic, and the comic experiences.
    d. Intellectual values. Values resulting from loving truth and finding truth.
    e. Religious values. Values developing from the feeling of satisfaction resulting from a dependence upon power beyond the individual person. Religion, is the reverence for and the worship of a power believed to be divine. It is a very important value in practically all persons.[80]

Naturalist Treatment of Values

There is a wide expanse between Christian realists and naturalists in their treatment of values. The naturalist believes values belong to human relations alone. The naturalist, not believing in any divine order, believes nature is indifferent to man and his needs and is not concerned with purpose.

For the naturalist, there is no other existence beyond this world. Values arise from and belong only to this world of human existence.

With this humanistic approach, it follows that values must be determined only by the scientific method. For the naturalist, the term is used in its narrowest sense, referring only to the physical sciences.

We are again confronted with the belief that "the end justifies the means." The standard of values is determined by the consequences. The value of an act can only be determined by the end product in the future. Values cannot be fixed or absolute. The naturalist denies any system as valid for all times. They must be related to the situation in which they arise.[81]

In a similar vein, logical positivists believe value or normative statements are not really knowledge statements at all.[82] For example, the statement, "A person ought not to steal," means, "I do not like stealing." This approach to value is embedded in America's cultural life-style. It reflects the teaching that we should not teach absolutes. It also supports the modern view that there is no such thing as "sin." This is an underlying belief of postmodern thinking. Without absolute truth, we are left with the societal accepted lifestyles that become broader and broader, and slowly encompass and condone every type of human relationship.

Genetic Theory of Values

Genetic theory deals with the problem, "When did values arrive and what was their origin?" Naturalists believe that values developed from primitive societies, out of necessity for group preservation. These early habits or customs grew, over time, into highly elaborate systems of values or codes of life. For the naturalist, the Scriptures are just a code of life that was developed through an evolution of development.

There are some glaring weaknesses in this theory. For one, according to this process, only values important to the group would have survived. However, this is not the case. Values harmful to groups have survived in some cultures for centuries. Values important for the survival of the group have perished in some cultures.

Related to these inconsistencies is also the problem of monotheism and polytheism. The evolutionary hypothesis teaches that polytheism came first, and then monotheism developed from polytheism. Archeological discoveries do not support this theory. Polytheism was a corruption of a primitive monotheism. Higher values (more favorable to the group) of a monotheist culture have often degenerated into the lower values (not favorable to the group) of a polytheistic culture.

Normative Approach to Values

Idealists believe values have an objective existence. Values are guided by ideals or norms that are objective.[83] In opposition to the naturalist, the idealist believes in a fixed standard of values for all time, a norm. The idealist comes close to acknowledging a supreme power. Edgar S. Brightman (1882-1961) wrote,

> "Idealists hold that ideals and values are not merely human standards and human experience, but they reveal the objective structure or cosmic purpose of the universe just as human sense experience and human standards of scientific method reveal the laws of nature.[84]

In this area of values, consider where you fit in; to what class of thinkers do you belong? What values are basic to your decision making process? All thinkers may be divided into two classes: either they are subjective or objective, naturalist or objectivist, Atheist or Theist.

Naturalists believe there is no realm outside of nature in which values could exist. Idealists believe nature is only the realm of the physical sciences and can only tell about one part of reality. The idealist believes that outside the realm of nature there exists, unchanging, eternal standards of value, giving order to our human existence, making values objective, not subjective.

Our Understanding of Mankind in Relation to Values

How does our understanding or doctrine of mankind relate to our view of values? There is a direct correlation between the naturalists, idealists, and Christian realists position on values and their understanding of the nature of man.

The naturalist believes mankind is just a part of nature, one of the higher animals. He is superior to other animals only because of a higher rational and spiritual nature (spiritual only in a physical sense), which is only more highly developed organization of impulses, perceptions and instincts common to all animals.

The only consistent value is that of constant change and development. Humanity is only responsible to maintain this position and strive for a higher value. Higher, only in the sense that it is relative to the time and that is justified by the end result. The very belief by naturalists that there is an order to development (lower animal to higher animal, polytheism to monotheism, poor values to useful values) implies some standard. The question is, who determines this standard of what is lower and what is higher? The very assumption of lower and higher flies in the face of their belief in the subjectivity of values.

Idealists hold that humanity is essentially divine. Humans are one with the divine and fully competent in the natural state, needing no spiritual transformation. All that is needed is intellectual growth and development. Humanity is considered able to independently realize values.[85]

Christian realism begins with God, not man; idealism begins with man and looks for God. Humanity is not one with the divine. The essence of God is eternal. Man was created from the dust of the earth. "The LORD God formed the man[B] from the dust of the ground and breathed into his nostrils the breath of life, and the man became a living being" (Genesis 2:7). Man is not competent in his *natural* state. "For who among men knows the thoughts of a man except the man's spirit within him? In the same way no one knows the thoughts of God except the Spirit of God." "The man without the Spirit does not accept the things that come from the Spirit of God, for they are foolishness to him, and he cannot understand them, because they are spiritually discerned" (1 Corinthians 2:11,14).

All persons require a transformation to understand and recognize value. Jesus said to Nicodemus, "I tell you the truth, no one can see the kingdom of God unless he is born again." Flesh gives birth to flesh, but the Spirit gives birth to spirit" (John 3:3,6). The apostle Paul wrote, "As for you, you were dead in your transgressions and sins" (Ephesians 2:1).

Human intellectual growth and development will not lead to an understanding of God. It may be used by God to draw us to Himself, but will not open the door of understanding apart from a spiritual transformation. John Wesley spoke of "prevenient grace." That is, God's spirit, even during our time of being dead spiritually, is still working and drawing us to respond to God's spirit, so we may be transformed. "For who among men knows the thoughts of a man except the man's spirit within him? In the same way no one knows the thoughts of God except the Spirit of God. " "For who has known the mind of the Lord that he may instruct him" (1 Corinthians 2:11,16)? Paul, in spite of his extensive learning in both Jewish and Greek philosophy and religion, wrote, "My message and my preaching were not with wise and persuasive words, but with a demonstration of the Spirit's power, so that your faith might not rest on men's wisdom, but on God's power so that your faith might not rest on men's wisdom, but on God's power" (1 Corinthians 2:4,5). Paul quotes from Job in the Old Testament these words: However, as it is written: "No eye has seen, no ear has heard, no mind has conceived what God has prepared for those who love him" (1 Corinthians 2:4, quoted from Job 28:7). "But the natural man (naturalists) receives not the things of the Spirit of God: for they are foolishness unto him: neither can he know *them (idealists)* because they are spiritually discerned" (1 Corinthians 2:14). But we (the transformed persons, from natural to spiritual, through Christ Jesus) have the mind of Christ.[86]

How the Christian Conceives Value

Basic to the Christian faith is the belief that mankind cannot realize true values apart from *new birth*. The natural man cannot discern the things of God; all truth comes *from* God.

The human natural mind is not capable of knowing truth about God, because of sin. Humanity is born totally depraved, separated from God by sin. When still in our natural state, by grace we are *born of God*, we receive the spirit of God and become fully alive, spiritual beings. In the new state, we are able to discern and realize values. As

John the apostle wrote, "But as many as received him, to them gave he power to become the sons of God, *even* to those who believe on his name: Which were born, not of blood, nor of the will of the flesh (naturalism), nor of the will of man (idealism), but of God" (Christian realism).[87]

Once we have received the spirit of God, it is still necessary to seek out God's intrinsic lasting values. The values of the Christian realist cannot be known apart from the spirit-directed reading of the Word of God. Scripture is the inspired revelation of God, from the very mind of God. When we begin to learn His truth, we will find that all true values are centered in the Glory of God. All true value is God-centered, not man-centered. The basis for all Christian values is the scriptural concept of love; love which has for its object, God Himself. In Scripture this is agape love, meaning a divine love. That love is implanted from Him; we cannot develop it, or find it apart from spiritual transformation.

Christian realism alone gives purpose to everything. It gives purpose to life: "for me to live is Christ." It Gives purpose to death: "to die is gain" (Philippians 1:21). It gives purpose to self: "I am crucified with Christ, nevertheless I live; yet not I but Christ lives in me, and the life which I now live in the flesh I live by the faith of the Son of God who loved me and gave Himself for me" (Galatians 2:20). It gives purpose to others: "Do nothing out of selfish ambition or vain conceit, but in humility consider others better than yourselves. Each of you should look not only to your own interests, but also to the interests of others" (Philippians 2:3).

Approaching Values Subjectively or Objectively

Subjectivity is simply that which is subject. It is that which is a servant, or slave of something or someone else. In an immaterial area, it is subject to the thoughts and feelings of the thinker.

Objectivity is a person or thing toward which action or feeling is directed; it is a purpose or goal for that directed action. It is external to the thinker, not controlled by thoughts or feelings.

In the sixties, I was a 6th grade teacher in Grand Rapids, Michigan. In social studies I led the class in a project to understand and discern subjectivity and objectivity in what we read. This was a time when it was still possible to see the distinction between news reporting and editorials in newspapers. The students were assigned to bring in several issues of the local newssheet. After guidelines in this exercise, they were directed to find objective written accounts (based on verifiable facts) and subjective statements (not verifiable by known facts) in the newspapers. They were to underline the objective statements with green crayon, and the subjective with red.

Amazingly, these young children, from many varied backgrounds, were able ninety percent of the time to make accurate assessments and differentiate between subjective and objective statements. The editorial pages were filled with red marks. We took it a step further; they were to now go home, and conduct this same exercise with their parents and bring back the results. The outcome was alarming; the ability to discern between subjective and objective material dropped to about forty percent!

The parents did not have the benefit of the training in the classroom, but I believe it says more than this. As we grow older, we do not automatically grow wiser. We are bombarded with data and without a basic understanding of our thought process, without purposeful training in how we think, subjective and objective statements merge like the varied hues of a landscape. Unfortunately, in our postmodern world, the idea of absolute truth has been trashed, which further leaves us adrift on a sea of confusion. If this experiment were to be conducted in the classroom today, I am afraid that the success of the students might reflect more the percentage of those adult parents.

Our postmodern world reflects this confusion of subjectivity and objectivity. Modern philosophy and the diminishing knowledge of the Scriptures has led to the absence of clear thinking, even among those who profess to be Christian in their faith. Comparison of the two terms can further be understood by the analogy of the servant and the king.

The servant's actions, virtually his life-career, is controlled by the king. The King is the object of the servant's obedience. The control exerted by the king will be less restrictive if the servant agrees with the standards (values) set for his or her conduct, and obeys voluntarily. Also, the servant's life will be a consistent life if the king's standards are followed (that is, assuming the king's standards are consistent).

Generally speaking, all thinkers fall into one of the two classes, subjectivists or objectivists. If a thinking person says values are subjective, that person, in effect believes mankind determines values. If a person says values are objective, that person believes values are external to mankind. The subjectivists are introspective –they look inward; the objectivists look out, and in some cases, look up.

Why do the subjective thinkers and the objective thinkers treat values in their respective ways? First, the subjectivist's approach begins with the assumption that there is no other existence exterior to, or superior to mankind. There is no other place to go to find values, other than mankind. The pragmatist is subjective, believing the best course of action is that which has the best consequence. There is no guiding principle or value to determine the action except the end itself. The end justifies the means if the end is the "best" end. Values are only relative to the situation; they are not fixed standards but only have value in relation to the worth of their end product. Since the end is in the future, the value is built upon something that may or may not come to pass.

No person can read the future. There are many so-called "psychics" and "fortune-tellers." Unfortunately, the only thing they can foretell is their own fortune made at the expense of the deluded people that are taken in. All the natural man can do is speculate. If values are set and actions determined by the speculation of the consequence of those actions, the values are built upon a foundation of "spec-ulative" sand. "The foolish man built his house upon the sand…"

Philosophy is integration of one's life experiences. The subjective view of values leads to a very narrow view of life. If a person's values are determined subjectively, not allowing for a source exterior to the person for direction, there is only a very narrow, subjective experience available by which to determine the correct values. A good example is the period following the war between the states. It was the time of the industrial revolution and big business development. The average working class had a very hard life. Their personal life experience showed nothing that indicated the working, guiding hand of an almighty God. What seemed to "fit: was "survival of the fittest" propounded by social

Darwinism. With much of the oppression of the era alleviated, many of the working class now have a different outlook on life. It has led to a different philosophy of life. Yet, in both good and bad times, subjective values are at the mercy of what is happening in the immediate environment.

We often can be in an environmental situation through which we only see "as through a glass darkly." Subjectivism of values gives little consolation or confidence to the person who is groping for a solid foundation. The subjectivist, especially in the promise of freedom from all restraints, offers to humanity what may seem secure but the disciple reaching out to embrace it finds only a mirage. For subjective values are built upon the reasoning and imaginations of the intellect, and what is more inconsistent and unstable than the mental state of the human mind.

Let us consider the objectivity of values in terms of a solid rock. The words, "solid as a rock" brings to mind the long-standing use of the Rock of Gibraltar as an advertisement for the Metropolitan Life Insurance Company. It is used as a symbol of strength, solidity, and virtually unchangeable. This author's first experience of viewing this massive monolith should serve to illustrate the stability and the life giving attributes of objective values.

As our ship, the USS Essex, approached the "Gates of Hercules," the entrance from the Atlantic into the Mediterranean Ocean between two continents, all new sailors strained for their first glimpse of the mighty rock. As the fog began to clear, on an early summer morning, the "Rock" came into view. What I did not know was the symbolic view in the insurance ads is seen only from the Mediterranean, and not the passage through the straights. What I beheld was a massive slope, which appeared to have large cement patching from top to bottom. Horrors! Is this symbol of stability crumbling and requiring concrete patches to hold it together?

Not the case. I soon learned the massive slope was a carefully prepared catch basin for rainwater that was channeled deep into the rock to provide a source of water for the population residing in Gibraltar. Out of the solid Rock came forth water to quench thirst. This so aptly illustrates the objective values that can only exist and be revealed by the divine creator. Paul, in his encouragement to the Corinthian church, compared Christ to the rock that was struck in the desert by Moses, from which water came forth for the traveling Israelites. Speaking of the multitude of Israel he wrote, "They all ate the same spiritual food and drank the same spiritual drink; for they drank from the spiritual rock that accompanied them, and that rock was Christ" (1 Corinthians 10:3,4). Jesus, in his dialogues with the Samaritan woman at the well, shared with her these words: Jesus answered, "Everyone who drinks this water will be thirsty again, but whoever drinks the water I give him will never thirst. Indeed, the water I give him will become in him a spring of water welling up to eternal life" (John 4:13,14). Objective values are solid like the Rock of Gibraltar, and give forth life-sustaining spiritual water.

The Christian realist builds the house of life on the Rock: "Therefore everyone who hears these words of mine and puts them into practice is like a wise man who built his house on the rock. The rain came down, the streams rose, and the winds blew and beat against that house; yet it did not fall, because it had its foundation on the rock." Unfortunately, most of the modern world follows only the subjectivism of humanity apart from the revealed objective truth of the creator. "But everyone who hears these words of mine and does not put them into practice is like a foolish man who built his house on sand. [27]The rain came down, the streams rose, and the winds blew and beat against that house, and it fell with a great crash" (Matthew 7:24-27).

The subjectivist believes that the values determined in the mind of man are the "best." Yet this same personage may determine in the mind that suicide is the best value, and jump from the safety of a solid stone bridge into waters below sealing their doom. The subjectivism of values is not a solid rock to the human mind.

The objectivist assumes the reality of the supernatural existence external and higher than mankind. The objective, Christian realist believes in the sovereignty of God, and that He is revealed in the Holy Scriptures. Through the Scriptures we can know the fixed values that can guide us and give our lives meaning and purpose. Only the objectivist has a "solid rock" spiritually. "The wise man built his house upon the rock – and it stood firm!"

Thinking Questions

1. What would you describe as the "highest good?"

2. How would you define "value?"

3. The word "value" is often used in today's communications. Discuss some modern day definitions of value.

4. Do you believe it is possible to establish value apart from God?

5. Are the Scriptures just a code of values developed over a period of time?

6. Do you believe all truth comes from God? Give a reason for your answer.

7. What prevents the human mind from understanding truth?

8. Is it possible to have true object statements of fact?

9. How would you characterize today's media, subjective or objective?

10. Is the content of Scripture subjective or objective?

11. Do you have a "world and life view" that integrates all of your life experiences?

Endnotes

78 Young, ibid, p. 123,124
79 Young, loc. cit., p.124
80 Ibid, p.125-126.
81 Ibid, p. 128.
82 Ibid., p. 129
83 Ibid. p. 130,131.
84 Ibid., p. 130,131.
85 Ibid., 134
86 1 Corinthians 2:16).
87 Ibid, p. 136, John 1:12,13.

12
The Problem of Purpose

The purpose-seekers of the world have approached this problem in many different ways. We want to look at two groups of thinkers, *mechanists* and *Teleologists*. Mechanists are just what the name implies, very mechanical in their understanding and believe nothing exists apart from pure matter. Teleologists believe that for all of life there is a purpose. The word comes from two Greek words, *telos* and *logos*. It literally means "the theory of ends."

Mechanism teaches that reality is a great and intricate machine, like an airplane or tractor, but is far more complicated. Reality is to be understood in terms of material atoms in motion.[88] Mechanism reduces every process of life to purely physical events, denying existence apart from matter. Mechanism denies that reality is an end-realizing process. It denies that living and creative processes are grounded in an eternal being. There is also denial that mind is a true cause in living things, and that life processes of plants, animals and humans differ in kind. Mechanism, pressed to the logical conclusions is a very depressing and hopeless view. Purpose is a non-entity.

Teleologists believe nature is dominated by purpose, and that ends are being realized in reality. The teleologist believes in an eternal being and that a difference in kind from plants and animals exists in humans. It is very interesting to note that the word spoken by Jesus on the cross –"It is finished"- is a derivative of the word *telos*. Christ's purpose for coming to earth was finished. The theory of ends for the Christian realist has its foundation in God's Word and revolves around the person of Jesus Christ, who by His death gave purpose to our existence. Without the understanding of God and the relationship to Him through the finished purposed work on the Cross-, we cannot understand our purpose. All purpose is grounded in the creator. "For by him were all things created, that are in heaven, and that are in earth, visible and invisible, whether they be thrones, or dominions, or principalities, or powers; all things were created *by Him,* and *for Him,* and He is before all things, and *by Him* all things consist" (Colossians 1:16,17).

Relating value and purpose

The position that the thinker holds regarding purpose certainly relates to the view of value. The mechanist, denying an eternal force that is directing nature toward an end, denies the objectivity of values. Since all reality is simply a complicated system of physical events, values are subjective, and nature is an end in itself. There is no higher purpose or fixed standard of values. Since nature is constantly changing –and this is the highest process- then values are only relevant to the situation at hand.

This is highly impractical even in normal life. Persons without purpose are ships without rudders, drifting aimlessly through life. In 1960, while crossing the Atlantic, my ship, a 40,000 ton, 900 foot long carrier, lost hydraulic control of its rudder. This great ship, "The fightinist ship in the fleet", was floundering, helpless until the control of the rudder was regained, and we could again move forward towards our destination. Nature without purpose lacks any reason for existence. It does not require values, but only the "survival of the fittest" which is not a value, but only animalistic instinct. For values to be objective they must be focused on an object, a purpose. Nature alone lacks an object for values, for natural existence apart from a divine creator is subjective and therefore subject to its own forces of nature.

The mechanist has arguments to support their mechanistic view of purpose, and believes this philosophy "adequately" accounts for the physical, biological, psychological, and spiritual order. They also believe it meets the demands of science and accounts for intelligibility.

The mechanist believes the only way to obtain knowledge of the physical order is by exact quantitative concepts. It is believed that the success of mechanism in the realm of the physical sciences warrants the belief that the method may be extended to all sciences. Following the subjective path, the mechanist believes there is no more purpose or meaning in the world than you put into it. Mechanists believe life is what it does. Behavior of an organism explains its life completely. The inner man is not explained, just ignored.

It follows that the mechanist believes study of behavior is an adequate definition for psychology. Believing behavior is all that exists in the process of life, the study of the soul or mind is denied. Consciousness is synonymous with existence; unconsciousness is nonexistence.[89] The mechanist-behaviorist simply asserts mind is unreal. Behavior is real and mind is ignored.

In the mechanist' view of life, the spiritual order is simply values or ideals. The values are subjective and relative to the particular situation.[90] Natural psychological processes determine "Set" values. Many believe mechanism is the only true scientific hypothesis, and that it will succeed in accounting for all the facts.

Intelligibility is synonymous with mechanistic terms. Any terms outside the realm of physical-chemical processes are unscientific. One can almost hear Paul proclaiming, "The natural man receives not the things of the Spirit of God; for they are foolishness unto him: neither can he know them, because they are spiritually discerned" (1 Corinthians 2:14). "His understanding is darkened" (Ephesians 4:18).

The teleologist teaches the purposeful interrelation of matter and life. Life is dependent upon matter but it cannot be reduced to matter. Interrelations of matter and life exist but the reduction of life to matter is not possible.

The apparent preparation of the universe for life, the interaction of living things upon each other, and the physical order suggest that intelligent purpose is at work. The Bible affirms this: "For since the creation of the world God's invisible qualities—his eternal power and divine nature—have been clearly seen, being understood from what has been made, so that men are without excuse" (Romans 1:20). There are so many essential conditions necessary for life to exist on our earth that it would be mathematically impossible that they could all exist in proper relationship and at one time simply by chance.

The world is in the right relationship to our sun. The crust of the earth is the right thickness, the depth of the oceans are the right depth for the presence of oxygen. If the crust of the earth were ten feet thicker there would be no oxygen, or if the oceans were deeper they would have absorbed carbon dioxide and oxygen.

The rotation of the earth is at just the right speed and the speed of the earth around the sun is correct for the maintenance of life. The relation of the earth to the right sun in thousands supports life on earth, by its size, density, temperature, and the distance of rays. The gases in our atmosphere are present in just the right proportions. The chance of any one of these factors (and there are many more) occurring would be astronomical; the chance that they would all occur together is too great to be calculated. The evidence is conclusive in favor of a supreme intelligence.

The theory that living organisms are evidence of adaptation to the environment is no longer tenable. The behavior of organisms cannot always be interpreted in terms of response to stimuli of the environment. Many times they act quite contrary to their environment. The organism is a whole that must be understood as a whole. It is not just a sum of its parts. You cannot take apart an organism and still have life. You can take apart a machine and still have all that it consists of. Higher forms of life have been produced that are not necessarily the best adaptation to the environment. A human baby, the highest form of life, requires expert care or it would perish.

Variations not only appear, they appear together in abundance. There are thousands of parts in the eye of the vertabra that cooperate to make the eye properly function. The mechanist asks us to believe these various elements that are variations, all fit in with each other, and yet not one single variation had anything to do with the others. The mechanists, seeing this problem, jump into the theory of leaps or mutations to explain it. How, may we ask, could this "leap" still produce an eye, coordinated in all its functions when even an infinitesimal change in one of the thousands of parts would make vision impossible?

We must address the relevance of thought to reality. The order of the mind and the order of things have a correlation that promises well for human adjustment. The intrinsic value of the intellectual capacity is often forgotten. Is the knowing process just an accident of chance?

A view of the idealist-teleologist leads them to a false view of nature. Ruling out any miraculous action on the part of a divine being, they believe that natural law is regular and dependable. Man has some freedom of choice but is certainly constrained by the Fall, sin having taken away the perfect relationship with God.

Human values are not man-made. Human values testify of the orderliness of nature. Nature is the objectivity of human values. Humans can and do develop or create their supreme value –*character*. Mankind is not a puppet; we are responsible for our actions. Humanity can produce either good or evil. This is a world in which our greatest task is to make the potentiality of value into actuality.

The universe has a moral order, just as there is a physical, biological, and psychological order. A specific course of action always brings a particular result.[91] Humanity cannot be indifferent to the world, for it is not indifferent to humanity. Values exist. There is definitely a moral direction to the universe.

Basic to all religious experience is the belief that a superior being exists, independent of the human mind. The very nature of religious experience points beyond the *experiencer* to God. If man believes in this being who is concerned with man and his creative growth and development of values, then it is common sense to believe this being will make himself known through religious experience.

Bankruptcy of Mechanism

Mechanists claim to adequately account for all physical, biological, psychological, spiritual, science, and intelligence orders. The mechanist's process reduces everything to the realm of science. It therefore becomes science and is no longer a philosophy of life. Mechanism does not give a complete synopsis of life except in the realm of science. Mechanists simply ignore a large portion of life experience and do not integrate all the facts. They describe life but they do not account for it. To properly *account* for life there must be an *accountant*. An able accountant not only describes data but is able also to explain the information. In the finite universe of our minds we can only describe life. Only a greater being, transcendent of the life we know can adequately account for life.

The Christian view of purpose

Christian realists agree that proof for the existence of God is not based on the study of design or purpose in natural phenomena. It is, however, certainly one of the methods by which the truth of that belief may be affirmed. It cannot, however, stand independently of the authenticating Word of God.

Apologetics (the study of defending the faith) has two major schools of thought: the *Dutch School* and the *Princeton School.* The Princeton School believes apologetics looks to reason as its mode or norm of operation. The task of the faith-defender is resolve of intellectual tensions. Apologetics is used as the *heavy artillery* to knock down the opposition and clear the way for the Word of God. This school would use the study of design and purpose as their their *heavy artillery.*

The Dutch School does not use apologetics as a mediation; they begin with God. The Word of God is the heavy artillery. This school's main spokesperson was Cornelius Van Til. Van Til presented Christianity as an authoritative religion. In other words, we cannot *prove* the Word of God for it is the *authority.* Nor can God be proven; we accept Him by faith. God confronted Moses in the desert at the burning bush. Moses asked Him whom he should tell the enslaved Israelites sent him? God answered, "tell them "I am" sent you. God is infinite and our finite minds could never prove an infinite being's existence. We accept God's word because it is God's Word, and accept God and believe that He is, because HE IS! The revelation of God is self-authenticating, and the Holy Spirit that comes to dwell in the hearts of mankind bears consistent witness to this truth.

Outside evidences such as the teleological argument are not part of the foundation of authenticating truth, but an integral part of the building itself. They are not supports. God, and God's Word support them.   "The Christian realistic philosophy must stand on its own foundation –the experiential conviction that God has spoken and made His purposes known."[92] "In the beginning God...and God said.." Jesus did not present to the Pharisees simply a rational argument; he spoke what was true and the Bible tells us they perceived that Jesus spoke as one having authority.

John R. Ingram

Thinking Questions

1. Are you a "mechanist" or a "teleologist" in your thinking? Consider this question very honestly; not what you say you believe but what you truly think.

2. Apart from what you claim as your belief regarding values, do you live your life supporting an absolute value system or a subjective value system?

3. Is study of behavior an adequate definition of Psychology?

4. Discuss evidence for intelligent purpose.

5. Does the ordered mind support a mechanistic or a teleological view of purpose?

6. Which method of defending faith do you believe is correct or is the most consistent with Scripture, the *Dutch School* or the *Princeton School*?

7. How is question 6 relevant to sharing faith?

Endnotes

88 Ibid , p. 139
89 ??
90 Ibid, p. 144
91 Ibid, p. 152
92 Ibid, p. 158

13
Natural Theology and Religion

Religion can be studied and defined in two major areas: *descriptive* and *normative*. Descriptive philosophy explains religion as experienced by the individual. Normative philosophical definitions endeavor to set forth religion in an ideal manner, as the particular philosopher believes it ought to be. Narrowly defined, religion is a service or devotion to a supreme being. Broadly speaking, religion may include the atheist for religion is worship of any object, whether it is God, money or nature. Anyone having an object of devotion is considered religious.

Methods of studying religion

Religion may be studied historically, experientially and philosophically. Historical study looks at religion in various cultural environments. The purpose is primarily descriptive. Experiential study is concerned with the individual's religious experience, and is studied both descriptively and normatively. Many Christians look at religion in a normative manner. Although believing there is only one *norm* based on Scripture, that norm takes many forms in the numerous denominations of Christendom. Philosophical study is an attempt to relate religious values to all of life as a whole. It is usually a man's religious conceptions that guide him in his outlook on life. Many have tried to write objectively in regard to the various philosophies, but guided by personal religious values, the views are usually prejudicial. Idealists believe no real religious philosophy may be attained unless one begins with an atheistic viewpoint.[93] The naturalists readily accept certain philosophies as religious while at the same time denying the existence of the supernatural.

Dealing with the problem of evil

The problem of evil will be discussed as long as there are people on earth. This problem is especially important to the Christian realist who believes we are living in a world controlled by a sovereign, perfect, good God. The presence of evil seems contradictory to this belief. Let's discuss evil in two categories or types, *natural* and *moral* evil. Moral evil is in relation to human personality, while natural evil is related to the natural order. For the latter, man is apparently not accountable, unless we delve into the improper use of the environment. Certainly, some conditions on earth have been brought on by the indiscriminate expansion and industrial projects of man.

Nature, it seems, is constantly waging a war on mankind, and mankind on nature. The recent tsunami of Indonesia, one of the greatest disasters in recent history, was a tragic destruction of life. Following shortly on the heels of this tsunami was the widespread earthquake throughout the regions of Pakistan. Then Katrina hit New Orleans, the most widespread disaster of the American shores. Such events are constant threats to mankind's existence. We cannot overlook also the tragic personal affects of the many diseases such as cancer, leukemia, and heart disease, to name a few. To the naturalist this is completely contrary to the belief in the supernatural, good-god. For the naturalist, these events of nature are not evidence of a perfect designer; they are only the workings of a mechanistic world, having no guiding purpose.

The terms "evil" and "good" to the naturalist only denote individual interpretations of given data. Evil is only mankind's term for natural failure and weaknesses. In the struggle for existence, "evil" and "good" are subjective terms, not objective, and are closely related to the naturalists' opinion of values discussed earlier.

The naturalist makes little distinction between moral and natural evil, for this system gives no basis for distinction. All matter, whether animate or inanimate, proceeds from the same source and moral evil in man is only the "influence of vestigial remnants of a brute inheritance."[94] All evil, whether moral or natural is simply rooted in a struggle for existence and is evidence of that struggle.[95]

Some idealists believe in a personal God. Yet, because of the existence of so much evil, both morally and naturally, they do not accept belief in an omnipotent god. The idealist believes that although morally good, the presence of evil in the world is evidence that the divine being is not able to control the universe.

Bertocci as an idealist believes these "facts" force us to believe God is finite. The Supreme Being is trying to control powers that did not originate from God. These powers appear to be defeating purpose in the universe for which God constructed it. The Christian realist asks, "How can Bertocci *know* that God's ends are being thwarted? The Scriptures tell us God's ways are past finding out (Romans 11:33).

Brightman endeavors to solve the problem of evil by postulating what he calls *the given* which is eternally in the very nature of God. According to Brightman, "the eternally good, creative will of God is being opposed by the non-rational "Given" within him. According to his theory, God may be thwarted, but he finds new ways of advance and forever moves on in the cosmic creation of new values. It appears that God is always *becoming* and never quite *arriving* at a state of perfection.[96] This is simply a case of finite minds that cannot conceive of anything or any god being infinite. To define God and explain evil as Brightman has done lowers the omnipotent, omnipresent, omniscient, eternal, holy, just, sovereign God to something little more than an imperfect, faltering man. Mankind, instead of recognizing the Creator, constructs a god not to be worshipped but to be pitied.

Bertocci's position is labeled "theistic finitism." Three points summarize the view:

1. The actual limitation of human ability.
2. The consequences of maladjustment, for man is physically and morally inadequate in many cases
3. The presence of natural evil that produces more harm than good.[97]

There are major objections to this theory. The values of unity, supplied by the doctrine of God are destroyed by finitism. If God is finite, it compromises the divine goodness and does not satisfy the demands of religious faith. If God cannot prevent evil how can He save from it? The very fact of creation assumes an infinite God. For if he knows creating this world would create evil He could not overcome, why did he create it?

Belief that most suffering is evil and irrational is dogmatic and is not consistent with biblical truths or scientific truths. Brightman attributed anything he did not understand to weakness in God rather than limitation of human knowledge by the sinful state. If God is limited in this way it is futile to cry out to Him for deliverance from evil. Such theists humanize God. They model him after their own being for that is all they understand. They accept nothing by faith.

If God has failed in overcoming evil in eternity past, what assurance is there that God will overcome it in eternity future? By present standards it appears God is losing the battle. The *given* theory of Brightman does not adequately explain evil, but only relegates it to the scrap heap of the unexplained.

Empirical evidence and natural theology

Is belief in an absolute or infinite god justified empirically? As we have explored many approaches to thinking in the philosophies of the world, it is quite apparent that all empirical attempts to demonstrate the existence of the supernatural have failed. Naturalists have identified three general lines of development in naturalistic religious thought.

1. Looking for evidence in nature of a theistic cosmology has resulted in evolutionary theism. This means that God is found growing within the natural process. God is evolving!
2. An interest in formulating metaphysics by facts of experimental and mathematical science results in cosmic theology.
3. Endeavors to formulate a philosophy of life to guide and inspire the strivings of mankind based on method and findings of science results in religious humanism. "Humanism is free from

any belief in the supernatural and dedicates itself to the happiness of humanity on this earth through reliance on intelligence and the scientific method, democracy and social empathy."[98]

Are there any "values" in natural theology? Certainly not anything that is constant or foundational. Religion in the individual life is viewed only as a means of broadening and enriching experience. For the naturalist, true religion is obtained by tolerance and moderation in one's search for religious values. "Tolerance" today means openness to anything but a belief in absolute truth.[99] For John Dewey, god is simply that drive that leads us on to the realization of ideals. Nature as a whole becomes the religious objective. Values such as salvation and immortality are denied or ignored by naturalists.

Another naturalist taught that god is essentially a process of growth that operates within human experience and brings about the development of values. God is just *creative activity.* For humanists, the proper study of mankind is man. They have shifted the theological and devotional emphasis from God to man, denying the existence of the supernatural. Man is worshipped as the object of his own religious life. "Be religious... but do not confuse the imaginative world of spirit with the *real* world of matter."[100] The heart of their worship is preservation of humanity. They equate religion with social action. Yet their own words demonstrate their idea of preservation of human society is "survival of the fittest" giving no hope to the weak. "It is crystal clear that it [cosmos or nature] is indifferent to man's welfare, that it pays no heed to his moral stature. Therefore, man need give it scant concern, but rather, as taught by humanism, must rely on himself for any betterment of his lot."[101]

Ultimately, the religious framework and function of naturalism is humanism. Their basic tenets are in complete opposition to the Christian realist beliefs. They deny-

1. God
2. Supernatural intervention in nature
3. Satan
4. Prayer and worship
5. Eternal life after death
6. No abiding self (the mind)
7. No Savior

157

8. No set moral order (subjectivity of values)
9. No social standards

They believe persons can rely on themselves.

Humanism's aim is to rid the world of every particle of supernatural religion, and set up, in its place, a humanistic religion, based on only those truths arrived at through scientific investigation, based on the belief that all nature has evolved, continues to evolve, and man is supreme.

Idealist view of religion

Personal idealism is theistic, but rests upon experience, not revelation. The idealist accuses the naturalist of finding their conception of values, not from their theories, but rather from within the culture in which they are reared. In the same fashion, the Christian realist accuses the idealist of finding many of their religious values from within the Christian revelational framework rather than from their experiential theistic philosophy.

Let us examine the idealist philosophy. First of all, personalism is metaphysical. They point to an object beyond the immediate experience. "Idealists insist that a real, personal, creative, and active god is the only being who can give a satisfactory account of man's value experience."[102] The moral will and the rational ability of man are the ultimate criterion of judging religious experience.

Personalism is a social religious philosophy. Man is made to work, not only with others about him, but also with God his creator in the production and conservation of religious values.

Personalism is a rational religious philosophy that rules out subjectivism, revelation, authority, and tradition as possible criterion of truth. This religion is built upon a coherent interpretation of all the "facts" of experience. Personalism is a mystical religious philosophy teaching there is in true religion the mystical quality of communion with God. Personalism does believe in immortality. The personal idealist believes God conserves values; he does not destroy them. Consequently, they believe that persons of intrinsic value must abide eternally.

There are many problems with idealism. If God is limited, how can man be certain of answered prayer or eternal life? If God's purposes are being thwarted, how can we be assured His will for our life will be carried out?

What is required for an adequate religion?

There are many forms of religion throughout the world. The Christian realist believes there is only one that is adequate and totally fulfilling– Christianity. Un-fortunately, biblical Christianity has been obscured and misrepresented by many elaborate forms of worship and activities, "having the form, but lacking the power thereof." A distinction must be made between the institutional church and the Christian faith. In the excellent book, "Letters from a Skeptic," a son responds to his father's skepticism about the atrocities that have been perpetrated on individuals and groups in the name of Christianity. "The fact that it was the 'Christian church' which chose to do the evils you write about, and to do them using God's name, in my mind only serves to show that all that goes under the name of 'Christian' is not necessarily Christian. Christianity isn't a religion or an institution of any sort: it's a relationship...people who have a saving and transforming relationship with Jesus Christ...the 'religion' of Christianity, the 'institution' of the church, is not itself Christian. Only people, not institutions can be Christians."[103]

An adequate religion is personal and satisfying to the individual. It is not a limiter of freedom; it gives freedom. Proof of this is seen wherever true Christianity is being practiced. So not only is adequate religion personal and satisfying, it is practical, and extends beyond the individual to other persons. In practice, Christianity works. With it comes full assurance of purpose in this life and eternity and joy in the next. This provides peace of mind to the individual in the midst of the difficult circumstances of this life.[104]

E.J. Carnell, in *"Philosophy of the Christian Religion" wrote,*

> "If one were to lay his finger on one of the most successful prejudices against the biblical faith, it probably is the fear that Christianity is an authoritative system of dogma which threatens to reduce the total complement of

values in a free individual. The hedonist fears reduction to a negative Sunday School manner of life, the lover of bread the choking off of material rights, the positivist the corrupting of scientific verification, the philosopher the imposition of an extra-rational revelation, the humanist the swallowing up of the dignity of man, the finitist the loss of goodness, the universalist the loss of love, the Roman Catholic the loss of authority, and the existentialist the loss of creativity."[105]

Such fears grow out of emotion and prejudice, not fact. Christ is the Good Shepherd. When He comes into our lives he brings abundant life and freedom. Freedom for non-Christians is often mistaken for license. This is not freedom, but a continuation and expansion of activity while still enslaved by the chains of the sinful state. Biblical Christianity defines and gives the stability and parameters in which we can grow in the self-creativity ordained by our creator.

Freedom is not having limitless boundaries. Without limits on the modern highway we could not experience the great freedom of today's travel. Without limits in areas of communication we would receive only garbled TV, computer, radio, wireless cell phone, and Ipod signals. Without limits children would have no freedom to grow up, and physical and sexual abuse –already epidemic- would all but destroy the possibility of any reaching a wholesome maturity. Contrary to the philosophers that see forms of chaos as the ultimate freedom, when the markers and parameters of moral existence are ignored, creativity is destroyed. Perhaps one of the most vivid real-world examples of this licentious freedom is the life of the drug addict. The religious existentialists were excited with the prospect of tearing down laws and norms, but as Carnell so graphically expresses, "the bleeding ankles of the captives now tell their own tale of suffering."[106]

We must understand that biblical Christianity defines a framework that supports the virtue of love and worth. Man-made legalistic Christianity has often been mistaken for the genuine article. The legalist' framework (based on pharisaical 'dos' and 'don'ts', attitudes of superiority and the insecurities of the natural man) is no more than re-worked humanism that pretends to embrace God and faith. The bible teaches there is only one true law within the framework of Christianity: The law of Love. Within this framework freedom is endless. God so loved the world that He gave his son to die for those who were still anti-God. Now, because of that divine sacrifice, we can love our enemies, a philosophy contrary to all other teachings on earth. This kind of love is impossible apart from the cross of Christ.

Anyone who wants to find fault in the Christian gospel can assuredly do so. But surely the rational person will at least acknowledge that satisfaction comes with the philosophy that answers the most questions and has the fewest difficulties. Christianity alone answers our deepest needs and resolves the search for relating faith and reason in the midst of the foibles of human existence.

Christianity has these distinctive characteristics:
1. Seeks to bring persons to decision.
2. Deals with the inward person, not just the external physical house.
3. Does not require human payment of works.
4. It is a personal religion and must be experienced personally.
5. Christianity cannot be achieved by simply knowing a set of facts. It requires an act of the will to allow an inward transformation of the heart by the workings of a transcendent Holy Spirit of God.
6. Christianity is not natural. It is supernatural, but is able to restore mankind to the quality of life intended by the God of creation.

It is impossible to know the qualities of relaxing in the warm soothing waters of a lake nestled in the beauty of a mountainous landscape without participating. So "no one can know the joy and complete adequacy of biblical Christianity save the one who has partaken...the whole gospel is adequate for the whole person."[107] Consider your thinking; are you ready to bathe your mind in the soothing waters of God's truth?

Thinking Questions

1. Has your faith become personal? Have you truly partaken of what you claim to believe?

2. What would be your *normative* definition of religion?

3. How would you describe the problem of evil as it relates to a sovereign, good God?

4. What does the term "evil" mean to the naturalist?

5. Consider Bertocci' view that God is finite. How did Bertocci arrive at such "infinite" wisdom regarding God?

6. Is it possible for a finite god to give assurance of a victorious future?

7. Are today's "values" considered absolute truth? If values are not constant, explain how communities and society can have any consistent standards.

8. Do values have to be constant (absolute) in order for mankind to not live in chaos?

9. For the humanist, who is God? What is the humanist' definition of religion?

10. State your requirements for an adequate religion.

11. What are the three ways to study religion? What are benefits and difficulties of each approach?

Endnotes

93   Ibid, p. 161.

94   Ibid, p. 166

95   Ibid

96   Ibid, p. 169

97   Ibid, p. 167

98   From a Pamphlet, "Purposes and Program of the American Humist Association, the American Humanist Association, Yellow Springs, Ohio.

99   Alan Bloom, *The Closing of the American Mind,*

100 Young, ibid., p. 176.

101 Humanism pamplet, loc.cit.

102 Young, ibid.,p. 177

103 Gregory A. Boyd, *Letters from a Skeptic,* Colorado Springs, Colorado, Kingsway Communications, LTD, 2003, p, 20.

104 E.J. Carnell, *A Philosophy of the Christian Religion,* Grand Rapids, Michigan: Eerdmans Publishing Company, 1960, pp. 512-516.

105 Ibid.

106 Ibid.

107 Ibid.

14
Empirical World Views

Definitions of naturalism and idealism

Naturalists are those who believe there is no support in experiences for a theistic hypothesis. While naturalists disagree on many points, they all agree on the absence of supernatural force.

Idealists are exact opposites of naturalists, believing there is ample evidence for the existence of a creative force or god. They do not necessarily believe in a transcendent god, nor an infinite god, but at least a force or guiding purpose. Just as the naturalists, the idealists also disagree among themselves on many points in their belief.

Agreements and disagreements of naturalists

The one belief by all naturalists is there is no supernatural. This point is assumed to be absolute fact. The basis of the assumption is similar to the circular argument of the evolutionists, building first the arbitrary geological scale, and then using it to support the evolutionary timetable. They assume that is a fact then build upon it the naturalist argument. The supernatural is ruled out and nature becomes "a kind of catch-all, a metaphysical garbage can, into which the naturalists may toss anything not to their liking."[108]

Naturalism is not a unified metaphysical system. It is simply investigative inquiry within an anti-theistic framework. This leaves a tremendous freedom to the naturalist and accounts for the many inconsistencies of their view.

Naturalists claim to follow a strict use of the laboratory method of investigation as used in the physical sciences. If strictly followed, this would limit the criterion of truth to only those evidences available and verifiable through the senses. Yet the strict form of methodology is not always followed and often becomes quite general. Naturalists believe they have agreed upon methodology from the Greek thinker, Democritus to Dewey, and have only varied interpretations because of varying historical conceptions of science. They view the changes as refinements in the process.[109]

Naturalists agree upon the "new" view of nature. The view teaches that atoms are not treated as indivisible -acting only in a mechanistic fashion- but are constantly in flux. Nature is no longer believed to be static and unchangeable; nature is always in process. The modern naturalists accept emergent evolution as the process of nature.

Naturalists agree that mind or consciousness is a quality that has emerged in the process of nature. It is just a higher form of existence in the emergence of evolution. It follows that they agree on the subjectivity of values, including of course religious values. Naturalists agree that reality is mechanistic, not guided or directed by any purpose, although purposeful beings emerge within nature. In the larger view, naturalists disagree on doctrines and teachings. Their methodology is consistent, but the conclusions reached are varied and contradictory. Contrary to their claim for consistency, these differences have reigned from Democritus to Dewey.

Evolutionary naturalism and pragmatism

Evolutionary naturalism is a term used by Wood Sellars to describe his own position. Sellars is not in mainstream naturalism, for he does not equate philosophy with science. He believes philosophy is a reflection upon the facts and concepts developed by the sciences. Sellars accounts for the presence of values and new qualities in nature by the theory of emergence rather than a personal force. He believes nature has within it a creative power. Sellars finds no proof for the supernatural, and writes, "There is no central, brooding will which has planned it all."[110] As with all naturalists, values are only subjective, not abiding in the cosmic order, but always subject to change.

Sellars position can be summarized as follows:

1. Rejection of the older materialism (reduction of mind and values) reduced to the level of physics.
2. Reality built up from eternally existing structure.
3. Explanation of mind in terms of physical process.
4. System of values related only to human life.
5. Conception of matter endowed with creative power.

Pragmatism is often associated with John Dewey's *Instrumentalism*. Pragmatism is the belief that if the right end is achieved the course of action was the right one. Truth is subjective and dependent upon the consequence of the action. Dewey believes a man does not think until confronted with a problem. Pragmatism's main tenets can be summarized as follows:

1. Organic character of nature.
2. New qualities emerge in nature by means of chance variation and natural selection.
3. Mind is simply an instrument of organic adjustment.
4. Truth is relative to the situation —follow the course of action that works.
5. The experimental method of the physical science is the tool of discovery, although this practice is not consistent.
6. The social situation can be changed and controlled by intelligent human guidance.

Vitalism

Vitalism is belief in a force within nature that accounts for the theory of emergence in evolution. The naturalists, having taken God out of experience, now find it necessary to bring back into experience some force to account for the facts. Chance and selection alone seem unable to answer the problem, since so many events have appeared in such perfect relation to each other as to defy the concept of chance emergence. This force is not God, but an impersonal vitalistic force with in nature itself. Perhaps, in some ways this could be deemed a form of pantheism. There are three advocates of *vitalism;* Henri Bergson, C.L. Morgan, and Alfred North Whitehead.

Henry Bergson (1859-1941) published his book, *Creative Evolution* in 1907. Bergson believed evolution was the basic fact of the universe, but it did not explain everything. He believed evolution needed a cause or otherwise the universe might have slept for eternity. He believed the movement (evolution) is due to a vital impulse (élan vital) that carries things forward. This impulse is creative and fresh every moment. The vital impulse creates its path as it goes, and there was no fixed beginning, nor a fixed ending.

C.L. Morgan (1852-1936) published *Emergent Evolution* in 1923. Morgan believed mind was a co-operator in the shaping of the objective world. The non-physic mind is unknowable yet believed to exist. Cognition clothes it with flesh and blood. He explained that new, unpredictable qualities and connections that arise in evolution were caused by a power operating in the universe.

Alfred North Whitehead (1861-1947) believed reality should not be interpreted in atomistic terms. "It consists of events which have their spatial and temporal aspects and, in addition, are the expression of the 'ingression' of eternal objects (universals) into individual instances, as illustrated by every assertion of identification in the form: 'This is a tree.' God is the system of eternal objects thus expressing itself I the actual universe, a process, not static in entity."[111]

Positivism

Positivism is one of the stronger and more active movements in the naturalistic school. This school movement insists all knowledge must be obtained through sense experience with the exception of mathematics.

All knowledge is positive or scientific; there is no metaphysical knowledge. All knowledge is sense; all else is non-sense. "The positivist passes over the question 'why?' in favor of the question 'How?' Natural laws replace absolute causes, for teleological explanations have been abandoned in favor of mechanism."[112] The positivist allows for only two types of statements:

1. Experiential verifiable judgments that are meaningful.
2. Metaphysical judgments that are logically true, whether the "facts" are true or not.

A main advocate for positivism is Auguste Compt (1798-1857). Auguste Comte was a student of Kantian philosophy. He believed Kant was right in limiting human knowledge to phenomena and declaring transcendental metaphysics impossible. He believed, therefore, that one should renounce all speculative philosophy and limit study to the definite results of science. Comte believed the evolution of mind is in three stages, from the lower to the higher, theological, metaphysical, and positive. "Theological is the stage of primitive culture, in which all events are explained by reference to the wills of personal beings. In the metaphysical stage, explanations are in terms of impersonal forces and general concepts. But in full maturity the mind discounts both of these and thinks in terms only of phenomena and their mathematical correlations."[113] In other words the highest level of mind is mechanistic mathematical science.

Absolute versus personal idealism

Absolutism says that reality is one eternally existing being. Everything that has existed in the past, exists now, and will come to pass in the future, is but some phase or aspect of the eternal and all-inclusive absolute. Hegel was an absolute idealist. Looking at history in this light he saw reality as a rational mind eternally in a state of process and development.[114]

Since Hegel concluded that the rational is real, and the real is rational, the conclusion is reached that all pain, all evil, whether natural or moral, is in essence good, rational and necessary. This makes it difficult to see how any real conception of obligation regarding morals (since there is not sin) can be maintained.

Nature is physically real, but in a metaphysical sense, it is only the external expression of the eternal consciousness of God Himself. God did not create the world *ex nihilo,* but out of nothing beside himself. Although reality is real, it is entirely mental or spiritual in character. Brightman believed that personalism is theistic and its criterion of truth is coherence.

Contrasting the two views of naturalism, absolutism is pantheistic; personalism is theistic. The absolutist believes all reality, physical and spiritual, is of one eternal existing being. The personalist separates reality from God, although claiming it is the external part of his eternal consciousness.

Panpsychism

Panpsychism teaches that reality is made up of infinite minds on various levels of organization.[115] There is no material atom for the panpsychist, only living, actively mental, entities. Some panpsychists are theistic, others conceive of God as within nature, or pantheistic. Whitehead was one of these.

G. W. Leibniz believed God existed outside of nature. He published his *Modadology,* which is often taken as the summary of his doctrine of substance. Leibniz analyzed all reality into units of force, replacing the inert atoms of materialism. These units corresponded to the infinitesimal points that were the limiting constituent elements in differential and integral calculus. He called these units monads. He organized all the monads from lowest to the highest, the highest being God, the monad of monads.[116] Leibniz believed the relationship of these units was logical, and they do not exist in space and time.

Naturalistic and idealistic logic

Although both naturalists and idealists claim their beliefs are based on experience, there is a vast difference in their conclusions. Naturalists try to show the fallacy of idealism by use of the empirical method, and idealists try to prove naturalists wrong by the empirical method.

The following are eight points brightman lists as points of debate between idealism and naturalism.

1. It is desirable that the universe be akin to man.
2. All data knowledge is personal experience.
3. Our only direct experience of causation is in the will.
4. Idealism is coherent with all the facts of experience.
5. Idealism correlates the known objects of thought.
6. Idealism gives the best account of interaction.
7. The objectivity of norms points to idealism.
8. Personalism is especially coherent with democracy and social aspiration.

A common theme in these two schools is the use of human intellect as their foundation. Both speak of criterion of truth, which fall back on mankind as a foundation. It is again, a prime example of the finite creature trying to define an infinite power by making it synonymous with nature (pantheism), separating it from nature but denying omnipotence and omniscience (theism), or ignoring or denying it altogether, limiting discovery to the physical sciences and mechanistic methodology.

Marxism: a Christian critique

Although the iron curtain as well as the Berlin wall and the cold war are history, Marxism is still alive and well in the world. It may be repackaged, but it still exists. It is an atheist philosophy underlying the direction of many "thinkers." A search of "Marxism" on the global Internet reveals 4,570,000 hits on Marxist articles. Searching "Communism" reveals 14,800,00 hits. This is exceeded seemingly only by the word sex. As one blogger wrote on the Internet, "I have not died. I am still alive. Imperialism and the enemy classes have not won me. I am still socialist and anti-imperialist." A joke, which is a non-joke goes like this: "There are no Marxists in the Soviet Union because they all found professorships in American Universities." Gary DeMar, in *Surviving College Successfully*, writes,

Marxist scholarship is commonplace in literary studies, sociology, anthropology, and history. In some fields, Marxism and feminism are the dominant worldviews of scholars. Between 1970 and 1982, four Marxist textbooks in American government were published. In the 1960s, only a few universities taught courses on Marxism; today there are over 400 such courses at universities around the country.[117]

Let us compare some basic tenets of this "religion" with Christianity.

Communism's founder, Marx, was a very impractical man, just as his philosophy is an impractical philosophy. He lived all his life upon money given to him by Hegel, his best friend, who was a very wealthy man.

In regard to reality, Marxism believes only in materialism; spiritual concepts are just the result of economic conditions. Christianity believes spirituality *is* reality, and material conditions are based upon spiritual truths. In application, Marxism believes economics determine moral standards. For example, if war is necessary to bring about the communist state, then war is moral. For the Christian, God sets moral standards.

In terms of the Supreme Being, Marxism does not believe in a supreme being, material is reality, and the state is supreme.

The one ethical imperative in Marx is to "overthrow all relations in which man is a debased, enslaved, forsaken, despicable being," with the ultimate end being to restore man to his true humanity from which he is alienated by capitalist society. In other words, Marx sees his purpose as teaching that "man is the highest being for man."[118]

Christianity believes God is revealed through creation and in special revelation –the Bible. For Marxism, spiritual truths are imaginary results of economic circumstances; there is no soul. Christianity believes man's soul is most important; the spirit lives forever. Our eternal state is the most crucial concern of this mortal existence.

Marxism is no friend of the family order. "Family" is only the result of economic necessity. Based on the Marxist foundation of materialism, man is not made in the image of God. We are social beings, with no individual nature. Christianity believes family is God-ordained, and a necessary building block of a moral society.

History, for the Marxist, is the dialectical process of material realities clashing with each other. Christianity, although accepting that mankind has freedom of choice in regard to spiritual decisions, believes God is sovereign over the universe and will determine the outcome in eternity. In this regard, Marxism does not accord freedom to the individual. "Freedom" is to act according to party policies for the good of the state. Christianity teaches acting according to the dictates of conscience directed by the working together of the Holy Spirit in relationship to God's revealed Word.

What does the Scripture teach regarding this philosophy or "religion?" The writer of Luke records that God condemns forced distribution of wealth: Someone in the crowd said to him,

> "Teacher, tell my brother to divide the inheritance with me.' Jesus replied, 'Man, who appointed me a judge or an arbiter between you?" Then he said to them, "Watch out! Be on your guard against all kinds of greed; a man's life does not consist in the abundance of his possessions" (Luke 12:13-15).

Charity is the responsibility of the individual: He who has been stealing must steal no longer, but must work, doing something useful with his own hands, that he may have something to share with those in need (Ephesians 4:28). Carry each other's burdens, and in this way you will fulfill the law of Christ (Galatians 6:2).

Jesus teaches that God is spirit, and is very *real*: "God is spirit, and his worshipers must worship in spirit and in truth" (John 4:24). The use of the Greek word for "spirit" in this context is qualitative, and speaks of the essence of God. It does not mean all *spirit* is God.

The Bible clearly teaches that material things can never satisfy. The spiritual realm is more important than the material. In Marxism, the focus on the good of the State and the general poverty of the masses seemed to teach the unimportance of material possessions, but there was no other goal since there was no believe in the spiritual realm. The State usurped the Biblical role of distribution of wealth and the role of the Church in society. Some forms of socialism are certainly communistic and have a foothold in Marxism.

In the Marxist view, persons who do not have a consciousness of their own supreme nature attribute the qualities that they lack to a being outside themselves. In this way, the idea of God is born. Every time a person loves God, it is a result of lacking love of self. It is much better to love "self" than the "idea" of God. To say, "I deny God means "I deny the denial of myself."

The idea of God is theoretically stupid since it is just the product of the imagination of a human being not yet conscious of his or her own divinity. Religion appears when "man is rendered as a stranger to himself." By crediting to another that which is rightly self, mankind distorts his or her true nature.

For the Marxist, human nature must be restored to itself. Identifying self does this by the attributes formerly attributed to God. Religion progresses as it suppresses relationship to God, and develops into a religion under a new form, the *cult of man*. Human nature passes from a negative to a positive state by the deliberate deification of mankind.

Marx says man has been alienated from himself or herself in two ways: 1) religion -by subordination to God, and 2) private property –by subordination to an employer. It follows in the Marxist "faith" that restoration and salvation is the destruction of both religion and private property.

The ultimate question for Marxism, as for any philosophy is, "Will Marxism satisfy a person at the end of their life?" The basic defect of Maxism is death. Death is the unsolved problem of communion because death personalizes. For a time the Marxist may feel like fruit on the tree of classless society. But he must remember that a day comes when the fruit falls from the tree. At the core of the fruit is a seed that prepares for another life. As death separated Dives of the Bible from his five brothers, so death separates students from their professors, and it separates every party member from the party. During life, force and terror and fear may extinguish personality, but death will reaffirm it.

There will be no attorneys to plead a person's case; no psychiatrist to plead they were not in their right mind because they did wrong; nobody to say he was not responsible because he had a complex; all the masks will be taken off; he will step out of the ranks and away from the crowd, left with only his consciousness. No Marxist will arise to defend him and say that he was determined by economic conditions and, therefore, was not free.

Standing in the day of judgment before the almighty God of the universe that one has denied all their physical life may be likened to an incident in the life of this author while serving in the Navy. While cruising among the islands of the Aegean Sea, our ship prepared for a nuclear attack drill. There were many "general quarters" drills, during which we donned battle gear and reported to our usual duty stations. My station was an emergency control tower station just aft of the ship's bridge, outside in a catwalk. In nuclear drills, all personnel had special stations inside the protective cover of the ship's steel bulkheads. When the alarm sounded for the drill, one sailor did not get the word: I proceeded to my usual station aft of the bridge. After plugging in my "sound power" headset and kneeling down at my station, it soon became obvious I was the only sailor in site for the 900 feet of our ship, fore and aft. Just as the awareness was dawning that I might be in the wrong place I turned and raised my head to look into the angled windows of the bridge, and found myself staring directly into the focused stare of Captain South, the commander of our ship. If it were possible I would have retreated into my steel helmet. There will be no one standing alongside of the atheist; each person will stand alone to give an account of his or her lack of faith.

One by one, as the scythe of death cuts down the ranks and allows the "I" to speak personally, communism meets its greatest enemy. Then shall stand the Christian message, "The most precious thing in the world is a soul that one day must go to meet its God."

The Marxist philosophy is diametrically opposed to Christianity, as it is totally atheistic. The beliefs of this philosophy dictate that Biblical faith must go. If communism were to conquer the world, they would be left with many of the population who have been brought up in a capitalistic and Christian environment. Unfortunately, in today's postmodern world, the latter may be less formidable.

Communism works by forming the character and personality of babies and children. Adults would already have established character and beliefs contrary to their teachings. As thoroughly materialistic scientists, they would not hesitate to say that they have no alternative other than disposal of these classes. They believe this would be justifiable homicide. Communism tries to regenerate human nature by education and edification of the person. They are also committed to destroying all traces of capitalism.

For the communist not one Christian or Capitalistic idea can remain in a person's mind. There must be completely new thinking. Communism only tolerates the Church as a means to an end. Under a communistic state, the Church must be destroyed to bring about the *Marxist defined* salvation of mankind.

Thinking Questions

1. What is the basic definition of naturalism?

2. How does the naturalist "new" view of nature conflict with the approach of the scientific world?

3. Is there an inconsistency in the naturalist' view that from a mechanistic, non-purposed process of evolution purposeful beings emerge?

4. What is the common belief held by all naturalists?

5. Is a pragmatic view of life ever acceptable? Can "The end justifies the means" ever be consistent with the teaching of Scripture?

6. Identify the inconsistencies of vitalism. Is vitalism simply an attempt to answer questions of purpose without acknowledging a purposeful god?

7. Is there any justification to deny metaphysical knowledge?

8. What evidence have you observed in your life or the world that points to a creative god?

9. What are the dangers of relying on sense experience as the only source of knowledge?

10. Explain how the use of belief based solely on the experience of the senses can lead to different conclusions.

11. All atheistic schools of thought, especially those grouped under idealism and naturalism, attempt to define some form of infinite power, whether it is pantheistic or mechanistic. What does this say about leaving a divine being out of the equation of human existence?

12. Do you believe Marxism is alive and well today, based on your knowledge of the present world conditions? Give support for your answer.

Endnotes

[108] Young, ibid, p. 183
[109] Ibid, p. 184
[110] R.W. Sellars, *The Next Step in Religion, p. 343.*
[111] Albert E. Avey, *Handbook in the History of Philosophy,* New York: Barnes & Noble, P. 270.
[112] Young, ibid,, p. 189
[113] Albert E. Avey, loc. Cit., p. 186
[114] Young, ibid., p. 194
[115] Ibid, p. 195
[116] Ibid.
[117] Stephen H. Balch and Herbert I. London, "The Tenured Left," Commentary (October 1986), pp. 44-45.
[118] Klaus Bockmuehl, The Challenge of Marxism: A Christian Response (Downers Grove, IL: Inter Varsity Press, 1980), p. 91

15
The Christian Philosophy of Life

Definition of Christian Philosophy

Christian philosophy is not based upon human intellect. The foundation of our faith is Jesus. "For no one can lay any foundation other than the one already laid, which is Jesus Christ" (1 Corinthians 3:11). The Christian realist believes truth cannot be attained apart from a supernatural revelation. This philosophy rests not upon the empirical evidence of man, but the disclosure of the existence of God through special revelation, the Word of God. This is *authoritative* philosophy. The *assumption* that the Bible is the revelation of God is supported by prophetic fulfillment, historic proofs, consistency with the spiritual nature of mankind, and spiritual witness within the heart of believers.

The cartoon that begins this chapter is from an early 1900's newspaper. It reflects an earlier era; a time when many philosophies were chipping away at the traditional Christian faith. The picture shows the swimmers, swimming off into the distance, to very unsure, dangerous waters. It is still an appropriate satire for the 21st century. More and more, even those professing faith in a Sovereign Lord are launching out into the world's seas without any sure mooring in God's revealed truth.

There is a leap of faith in every philosophy. I believe the leap is the shortest in Christianity and may not be a leap at all when we consider the evidences of creation and the witness of the Holy Spirit within our lives when we take that step of faith. The Word of God, the special revelation from the Creator, has been put to the test throughout the history of the world. It has not failed us; it stands authenticated by the witness of history and archeology. *In the beginning God"* is assumed. It is not rationalized; it is simply accepted by faith. However, our faith is "self-authenticating." That is, experience in the life of the believer through the witness of the indwelling Holy Spirit of God bears witness to the truth of God's Word. This chosen philosophy of faith is also the most consistent with all of life's criterion and experience.

There are many Christians who shrink from the term *philosophy,* believing it should not be associated with Christianity. This belief grows out of the misconception that philosophy only deals with the realm of empirical data and "rationalistic systems." This concept relegates Christian faith to the changing seas of emotions. True philosophy is integration of one's life experiences and the understanding of one's purpose in life. Christian philosophy differs from all others in that it is based not on human intellect, but divine disclosure. Apart from divine disclosure, "special revelation," it is impossible to construct a good life-encompassing philosophy. The truth disclosed in God's Word, centered on Jesus Christ, gives meaning and purpose to an otherwise meaningless and useless existence.

Revelation in the Christian World View

Christian realistic philosophy begins with the conviction of special revelation –not only does God exist but we know of His existence because He has made himself known to us. The heart of that revelation is to be found in Christ, the "Word who became flesh." The record of God's special disclosure is to be found in the written Word –the Holy Scriptures. Christian philosophy begins with the assertion of a positive, supernatural and authoritative message. This message is a divine gift, a Word that comes to mankind from beyond his or her own existence. If this basic belief is rejected there is no basis for building a Christian philosophy.

Christian Philosophy and coherence

It is seldom possible to convert a person from one philosophy of life to another by proving that the latter philosophy is the most logical. Christian realists believe their philosophy is the most coherent, based on certain assumptions accepted as factual. Those assumptions are the existence of God and special divine revelation of Him through the Scriptures.

Adherents to any philosophy accept their viewpoint as the most consistent or rational because they believe certain basic assumptions. In seeking converts to Christianity the problem is not proving faith to be rational, but leading a person to accept the basic assumptions.

Christianity is absurd for anyone who accepts the assumption that there is no supreme being. The work of conversion is the combination of the Word of God and the work of the Holy Spirit. Just as finite creatures, we cannot totally understand the infinite mind of God or create physical life, so we cannot bring about spiritual life through human means; it is the Work of God.

Christian Philosophy and Experience

Every world-view is experiential. The Christian world-view begins with a vital experience, a firm, deep conviction. The Christian world-view differs from other philosophies in one major aspect: the experience carries with it the conviction that it is not grounded in the natural order, but in God, the supernatural order, working through his spirit.

Philosophy must give a coherent account of experience as a whole. The Christian realist must take into account his personal experience of God in Christ Jesus. From the perspective of the Christian realist, accepting the Gospel of the Lord Jesus Christ is the only complete and coherent view of all life.

What the experience of the Christian is based on has long been a subject for debate. Does he receive this purely through faith apart from reason, or is it a combination of faith and reason? Christianity is not an irrational philosophy, but its roots begin in the commitment of faith. The writer of Hebrews says, "And without faith it is impossible to please God, because anyone who comes to him must believe that he exists and that he rewards those who earnestly seek him" (Hebrews 11:6). There are many evidences that can lead us to the faith to believe. The Bible speaks of the evidence of creation as a panoramic display of His existence.

> The heavens declare the glory of God; the skies proclaim the work of his hands. Day after day they pour forth speech; night after night they display knowledge. There is no speech or language where their voice is not heard. Their voice goes out into all the earth, their words to the ends of the world" (Psalm 19:1-4).

The gospel as presented in the Scriptures is foolishness to the natural man. Paul writes to the Corinthian church, "For the message of the cross is foolishness to those who are perishing, but to us who are being saved it is the power of God" (1 Corinthians 1:18). Original sin brought spiritual blindness to mankind. That blindness must be pierced with the spiritual light of the Gospel before the Christian message is perceived to be rational.

God did not devise a plan of redemption that could not be perceived and grasped by fallen man. John Wesley's "prevenient grace" (God's spirit seeking us before spiritual rebirth) is perhaps the best explanation of how God seeks every person. The natural revelation of God (creation) is evident to every human, and is used by the tugging of the Spirit of God on the heart of unregenerate persons to draw them to an understanding of salvation. The special revelation of God (Scripture) in conjunction with the Spirit of God brings about regeneration of the human spirit. The accord and affirmation found in this new relationship is the verification of Christian realism.

Relationship of Faith and Reason

Throughout the history of the Church there have been both balanced and extreme positions held regarding the relationship of faith and reason. Reason to the exclusion of faith tends towards rationalism, or what I would term a "mechanical faith." Faith to the exclusion of reason tends towards fanaticism. Faith plus reason is a balanced view regarding the Christian life.

Reason cannot be divorced from faith. Reason relates to mankind's intellectual faculty, which God created. It is the God-designed creative mind that is able to grasp the truths of God and respond in faith to the Holy Spirit.

Faith apart from reason is often the approach of the glitzy media presentation of the Gospel. Some telli-evangelists razzle-dazzle us with their high-speed presentations that offer no sense of reason, only the evil of not responding to their particular brand of faith. Many "prosperity gospel" sideshows are on national networks teaching that a "seed faith" sown to their ministry will produce monetary wealth for the giver. Others hawk instant healing if you just have enough faith. Hebrews tells us that "faith is the substance of things hoped for, the evidence of things not seen" (Hebrews 11:1), but this is not excluding the rational mind from the walk of faith. Paul wrote to the Roman church, telling them "to not conform any longer to the pattern of this world, but be transformed by the renewing of your mind. Then you will be able to test and approve what God's will is—his good, pleasing and perfect will" (Romans 12:2). The word "mind" is the *reasoning mind*. God is interested in whole, complete persons, body, soul and spirit. He wants us to be totally transformed and utilize the mind we have been given. We have been created in His likeness, to be creative, thinking, active free persons.

Conversion -acceptance of the Gospel- is purely an act of faith, and brought about by the regeneration of the Holy Spirit in our spiritually dead hearts. At the point of conversion, we act on faith. Before making that true commitment we have undoubtedly gone through a reasoning process.

I remember a graduate student at Wheaton College, who shared his experience of missionaries coming to minister at his village in Africa where he grew up. He would attend the services, where he heard about Jesus Christ. At the end of the service, the missionary would ask them to bow their heads and close their eyes, and not to look around during the invitation to receive Christ. As a young man, he would peek through his fingers, thinking God was going to appear in their midst. His people came again and again to hear the message, listening to all that the missionary had to say. They might do this over a period of weeks and months. After they had gathered all the information about Christ, and had decided that it was true, their way of responding was openly, standing up in the midst of the service, and declaring that they would follow Him. His way demonstrates the way of faith; not hiding and covering our eyes afraid we might actually see someone respond to Christ; but a carefully reasoned acceptance by faith, not a response to fervent emotional appeal.

Central Teachings of the Christian Philosophy

The foundation of the Christian world-view is the existence of a God who has revealed himself in a unique fashion. The record of this revelation is set forth in the 66 writings of the Bible. The culmination of this revelation is found in the person of Jesus Christ, God incarnate, whose entry into the world of mankind is described, as "the Word became flesh." In the present age God is present in the Holy Spirit. Although the Christian realist is monotheistic, believes in one god, the Supreme God is believed to be a tri-personal Godhead, God the Father, God the Son, and God the Holy Spirit. The Christian view of the trinity is not stated in Scripture; it is based on the attributes ascribed to the three persons of the godhead. These three persons of the godhead are mentioned in Jesus' great commission to his disciples before he ascended back into heaven:

> "Therefore go and make disciples of all nations, baptizing them in the name of the Father and of the Son and of the Holy Spirit, and teaching them to obey everything I have commanded you. And surely I am with you always, to the very end of the age" (Matthew 28:19,20).

God is in one sense the Father of all persons, in that He is their creator, sustainer, loves them and wants to draw all persons unto Himself. This does not mean all men are "children of God." Only through accepting the Son as Savior are they born into the *family* of God. Jesus made this very clear in his dialogue with Jewish religious leaders, who thought they were God's children. They claimed that relationship and inheritance by identifying their genealogical connection to Abraham: "Abraham is our father," they answered (John 8:39).

Jesus' response identifies the spiritual relationship necessary to truly be considered "God's children."

> "If you were Abraham's children," said Jesus, "then you would do the things Abraham did. As it is, you are determined to kill me, a man who has told you the truth that I heard from God. Abraham did not do such things. You are doing the things your own father does."

"We are not illegitimate children," they protested. "The only Father we have is God himself."

Jesus said to them, "If God were your Father, you would love me, for I came from God and now am here. I have not come on my own; but he sent me. Why is my language not clear to you? Because you are unable to hear what I say. You belong to your father, the devil, and you want to carry out your father's desire. He was a murderer from the beginning, not holding to the truth, for there is no truth in him. When he lies, he speaks his native language, for he is a liar and the father of lies. Yet because I tell the truth, you do not believe me! Can any of you prove me guilty of sin? If I am telling the truth, why don't you believe me? He who belongs to God hears what God says. The reason you do not hear is that you do not belong to God" (John 8:39b-47).

So God is Father in a specific sense, only to those who accept Jesus as their savior. God the Son, Jesus Christ, is truly God, incarnate in human flesh, with all of God's attributes; he is not just a man with unique power.

The Holy Spirit, the third person of the godhead, has a different office, but is truly a person, as much as God the Father. He is the person of the Godhead who is present today, working in the life of every true believer. Jesus promised the coming of the Holy Spirit in his instruction to the disciples before his crucifixion. The Spirit is the teacher and instructor of all believers.

But the Counselor, the Holy Spirit, whom the Father will send in my name, will teach you all things and will remind you of everything I have said to you (John 14:26).

Contrary to the naturalists and all the philosophers who deny the existence of a supreme being but have no answers as to origins, all things have been created by God and are dependent upon Him. God created *ex nihilo* –out of nothing. Material substance is not a part of God, nor was it ever a part of God; He created it.

Creation is a truth of revelation. Although there is much evidence, and corroborating support in nature and in the historical record, there is no absolute proof that the universe was created apart from the statements of God's Word. Creation implies the reality of time. Time is not illusory, but is actually taking place. God Himself is timeless, infinite, never changing. The existence of creation teaches that God has a plan and purpose in view.

Man is the goal of creation. Man is a rational and moral being. We are complete spiritual personalities, even as God; one person, but made up of body, soul and spirit. We have been created in the image of the creator which means we were created not by chance, or evolved into what we are today, but were created as rational, moral, and therefore responsible beings.

Moral evil had its origin in the fall of man. It is not unreal or illusory. The Serpent, Lucifer, initiated the temptation with that same deceitful lie.

> Now the serpent was more crafty than any of the wild animals the LORD God had made. He said to the woman, "Did God really say, 'You must not eat from any tree in the garden'?" The woman said to the serpent, "We may eat fruit from the trees in the garden, but God did say, 'You must not eat fruit from the tree that is in the middle of the garden, and you must not touch it, or you will die.'" "You will not surely die," the serpent said to the woman. ⁵"For God knows that when you eat of it your eyes will be opened, and you will be like God, knowing good and evil" (Genesis 3:1-5).

The deceiver planted the seed of temptation, and the woman was drawn into the deceit:

> When the woman saw that the fruit of the tree was good for food and pleasing to the eye, and also desirable for gaining wisdom, she took some and ate it. She also gave some to her husband, who was with her, and he ate it. Then the eyes of both of them were opened, and they realized they were naked; so they sewed fig leaves together and made coverings for themselves (Genesis 3:6,7).

This incident was the beginning of moral evil, mankind's revolt against the creator-God.

Moral evil does not exist by divine *design*, but only by divine *permission*. God could judge mankind immediately for their sinful state but He is long-suffering. Sin brings the judgment of death, but God has a plan. "The Lord is not slack concerning his promise, as some men count slackness; but is longsuffering to us-ward, not willing that any should perish, but that all should come to repentance" (2 Peter 3:9 KJV). God only tolerates sin because His plan is not finished in winning mankind back to Himself. All present evil is the fruit of the Fall, the initial act of rebellion against God. This moral evil is only removed through Christ's propitiatory sacrificial death on the cross in payment for the sins of the whole world. Dr. Arthur Williams, former dean of the Bible Department of Cedarville College often repeated this principle: "Christ's sacrifice was *sufficient* for the sins of the whole world; it is *efficient* for those who believe." We must choose.

Natural evil is real, not illusory as maintained by the teachings of "Christian Science." All natural disorders, including disease and pain are very real. Evil in its entirety cannot be accounted for by mankind's present activity.

Why did God create a world in which it was possible for moral and natural evil to appear? God in His sovereignty could have created mankind to of necessity be good. This being would not have been a moral being; this creature would have been merely a puppet with no freedom to act contrary to the will of his creator. Why did God not make beings incapable of suffering? For the same reason that He did not create beings that had to be good, he created living tissue, a living body that was capable of *feeling*.

Not only mankind, but also the whole of creation has felt the affects of the Fall. The Bible states the Fall affected even the earth by the appearance of weeds.

"Cursed is the ground because of you; through painful toil you will eat of it all the days of your life. It will produce thorns and thistles for you.." (Genesis 3:17b, 18).

Even the pain endured by women in childbirth is a result of the Fall.[119] God did not willingly plan evil but he permits it because of human freedom. Not the worldly idea of freedom to arrogantly throw off the restraints of spiritual truth, but the freedom to make a choice to return to the creator or be condemned to a life of anguish and eternal separation from God.

In spite of God's permission of evil, it does not thwart His divine purpose; He turns natural evil into His purpose. God declares through the prophet Isaiah, "I form the light and create darkness, I bring prosperity and create disaster; I, the LORD, do all these things" (Isaiah 45:7). Joshua records, "If you forsake the LORD and serve foreign gods, he will turn and bring disaster on you and make an end of you, after he has been good to you" (Joshua 24:20). The term disaster in the Hebrew stands for natural evil, calamity, adversity or affliction. The biblical writers always viewed natural evil as a means by which God could bring His purpose to pass.

I believe it is important to take time to clarify some misconceptions in terms of both original sin as a result of the Fall, and the indirect affects of sin bringing about natural evil, or affliction. Today, many purveyors of a religious message want to extend the hope to every person who is afflicted in some way that sin is the direct cause of their circumstance. So that by confession of sin, and seeking God, all sickness and disease can be cured. We are all affected by the fall in natural ways. We are all susceptible to the affects of a fire, a tornado, a hurricane, or the many diseases of the body. Can God protect us from natural disaster? Of course! Can God cure us from natural disease? Of course! Does He always choose to protect us or cure us? No.

The dialogue between Christ and His disciples when they encountered a blind man illuminates the thinking of the religious leaders at the time of Christ and many present day leaders. The disciples asked, "Rabbi, who sinned, this man or his parents, that he was born blind?" (John 9:1b, 2) Jesus clarified for them that the blind man was affected by the natural order; it was not a result of immediate personal or family sin. God had permitted it so the blind man could be blessed by the work of God as a witness to others. "Neither this man nor his parents sinned," said Jesus, "but this happened so that the work of God might be displayed in his life" (John 9:3-5).

In Christian philosophy, the problem of evil is overcome by redemption through the reconciliation of mankind with God. The reconciliation takes place through the Son, Jesus Christ, who came into the world (became flesh) for this purpose.[120] Modern philosophies view the life of man as a steady upward climb out of the slime pits as he overcomes the influence of his brutish ancestry. The Christian philosophy believes mankind fell from a higher state into the slime pits and needs to be restored. Rather than a history of development and growth, man has a history of degeneration.

All philosophies have a theory concerning human destiny. These are the main philosophical arguments advanced for immortality:

1. Universality of the belief.
2. Man's nature is so great as to call for better things than the present existence.
3. Man is so made that he must rise to greater heights spiritually than provided in this present world.
4. Man's present existence is incomplete, so a future age is required for his development.
5. Man does his best when the hope of a future existence is always before him.

These arguments prove little except show that belief in future life is widely held.

The promise of immortal existence is the great hope of the Christian philosophy.

1. It is built on the biblical view.
2. It is implied in the biblical doctrine of man. He was made for eternity.
3. The separation of body and soul is viewed as unnatural.
4. The supreme evidence for the Christian hope is to be found in the resurrection of Jesus Christ.

The Christian philosophy, then, is centered in Christ. In Revelation, we have the prophetic picture of the followers of the Lord in a Christ-centered picture around the throne in heaven:

> "they are before the throne of God and serve him day and night in his temple; and he who sits on the throne will spread his tent over them. Never again will they hunger; never again will they thirst. The sun will not beat upon them, nor any scorching heat. For the Lamb

at the center of the throne will be their shepherd; he will lead them to springs of living water. And God will wipe away every tear from their eyes" (Revelation 7:15-17

The Value of Philosophy for Christians

The idea or belief that Christianity is not a philosophy is false. Those who would state this know little of Christianity or little of philosophy. Christianity is the only philosophy that has a true unifying principle to offer mankind. Christianity is the only philosophy that has answers for the problems of our human existence.

Our world today is one of extreme tensions in part brought on by the tremendous technological advances of recent years. This has brought the world closer together, so that the problems of the entire world lay at our fingertips. Satellite-provided television and the global Internet bring news and world situations into our homes daily at lightning speed. Now with ipods, cellular phone service complete with pictures, we are never away from a barrage of communication. To meet the anxieties, the fears, the problems of this postmodern world Christianity must be practical for today, not just a hope for life after death.

The Scriptures clearly teach it is practical for everyday life. Unfortunately, the Christianity that much of the world sees is all talk and no action. We have a responsibility to serve mankind, a responsibility to carry the gospel of Jesus Christ to the world, not just in word, but also in deed. Christ must be seen in us. John Wesley lived almost the entire eighteenth century in England, traveling over 250,000 miles on horseback to carry the gospel into the remotest and humblest regions. Moderately wealthy, he gave away most of his money to free many from debtors prisons. It can be truly stated, that he, almost single-handedly, transformed England, not just in spiritual awakening, but in the elevation of the standard of life for the vast poverty stricken populace.

To be equipped for the task of spreading the gospel, the Christian must know the people with whom he or she is dealing. We must know their ideas, their ideologies, their way of life as well as their life-situations.

191

Only then can we meet them on their ground with the gospel. One cannot communicate with a foreigner speaking a different language without speaking their language, nor can one help a person or give scripture applicable to their needs and ideologies if we do not understand their way of life. Remember, the Word of God is not a guide to excellence in spiritual performance; it is God's relational direction to the freedom and exhilaration of standing before God with an unashamed and open pure heart.

The individual must write the final chapter in any book concerning the Christian philosophy of religion. The only way to gain knowledge of the person of Christ is to believe and partake. Proxy cannot generate friendship. Heart must meet heart in personal love. Knowledge by assumption must pass over into knowledge by consumption. In no other way can the values of fellowship with Christ be fully understood. Christian philosophy may show a path to God's love, and how spiritually gaunt a person will be who lacks that love, but it cannot make a contented lover of the person. Only the spirit of God can implant a heart of love, and only the rational will of the individual can summon the Spirit. We can know the meaning of any true value; it simply requires exercise of the will. To those of you who already profess this Christian philosophy, I challenge you with these words from the brother of our Lord:

> "My brothers, if one of you should wander from the truth and someone should bring him back, remember this: Whoever turns a sinner from the error of his way will save him from death and cover over a multitude of sins" (James 5:19,20).

Consider your life direction. "What are you thinking? Could there be any greater focus and directed purpose for our lives than a commission that involves our eternity and the eternity of everyone we meet?

There has been only one faith, one personal faith in the man Christ Jesus, which is able to fill the void felt inside of every human being. Only one faith that can turn disappointment into excitement, turn the depression of the mind into the creativity of exciting life, bring peace in the midst of heartache, and bring each living soul to the place of living not somehow, but triumphantly.[121] It is that focus in our lives, employing both our rational mind and our heart, that can guide our thinking and integrate all of our life experiences. A verse in Revelation, the last book of the Bible, gives us a vivid description of being Christ-centered: "For the Lamb at the center of the throne will be their shepherd; he will lead them to springs of living water. And God will wipe away every tear from their eyes."[122]

We began this journey with personal insights; I would like to end it with a personal note. The contemporary duo of Brooks and Dunn recently recorded a song, "Believe." It is a simple, yet profound statement that ascribes to life beyond our physical existence, life clearly defined by Christ in his words, written in red.

> Old man Wrigley lived in that white house
> Down the street where I grew up
> Momma used to send me over with things
> We struck a friendship up
> I spent a few long summers out on his old porch swing
>
> Says he was in the war when in the navy
> Lost his wife, lost his baby
> Broke down and asked him one time
> How ya keep from going crazy
> He said I'll see my wife and son in just a little while
> I asked him what he meant
> He looked at me and smiled, said
>
> I raise my hands, bow my head
> I'm finding more and more truth in the words written in red
> They tell me that there's more to life than just what I can see
> Oh I believe
>
> I can't quote the book
> The chapter or the verse
> You can't tell me it all ends
> In a slow ride in a hearse
> You know I'm more and more convinced
> The longer that I live
> Yeah, this can't be
> No, this can't be
> No, this can't be all there is[123]

Thinking Questions

1. What criteria external to the Bible supports the assumption that it is the revealed Word of God?

2. What is the "self-authenticating" aspect of the Christian faith?

3. How does consistency between life and faith support the Christian belief?

4. If you are not a Christian, what philosophy that is consistent with all of life's experiences have you adopted?

5. Name two aspects of the Christian philosophy not shared by any other philosophy or religion.

6. Can a logical argument ever convince anyone to accept the Christian faith?

7. Whatever your view of life, attempt to build a coherent view of life apart from any divine disclosure or greater divine being. Support your view with data you have received from the senses

8. Give your view of the relationship of faith and reason.

9. For you personally, what is the most important central teaching of the Christian Faith?

10. If you knew this was your last three months of life, what would you write as the final chapter regarding your personal faith ?

Endnotes

[119] Genesis 3:16

[120] Young, ibid.,p. 219

[121] Dr. V. Raymond Edman, former President of Wheaton College spoke these words. Dr. Edmond, now deceased, said, "Never doubt in the dark what God has shown you in the light."

[122] Revelation 7:17

[123] Copyright 2005 Sony/ATV songs LLC, Showbilly Music and Big Loud Shirt.